Happy
CACTUS

Senior Editor Bob Bridle

Editor Laura Bithell

Project Art Editor Louise Brigenshaw

Senior Art Editor Alison Gardner

Editorial assistance
Jo Hargreaves, Jane Simmonds

Design assistance Natalie Clay

Senior Jacket Creative Nicola Powling

Jacket Co-ordinator Lucy Philpott

Pre-production Producer
Becky Fallowfield

Senior Producer Ché Creasey

Creative Technical Support
Sonia Charbonnier

Managing Editor Dawn Henderson

Managing Art Editor
Marianne Markham

Art Director Maxine Pedliham

Publishing Director Mary-Clare Jerram

Illustrations Debbie Maizels

Photography Peter Anderson

First published in
Great Britain in 2018 by

Dorling Kindersley Limited,
80 Strand, London WC2R ORL

Copyright © 2018
Dorling Kindersley Limited
A Penguin Random House Company

2 4 6 8 10 9 7 5 3 1
001–310290–Mar/18

A CIP catalogue record for this book
is available from the British Library.
ISBN: 978-0-2413-4109-4

Printed and bound in Slovakia

A WORLD OF IDEAS:
SEE ALL THERE IS TO KNOW
www.dk.com

Happy CACTUS

CHOOSE IT, LOVE IT, LET IT THRIVE

Consultant **JOHN PILBEAM**

CONTENTS

FIND YOUR PLANT

With specific information and care details
for 105 different cacti and succulents,
this section provides everything you
need to treasure your prickly plant
and keep it happy.

Top five:

PLOVER'S EGGS
Adromischus cooperi
pp.32–33

FLAT-TOPPED AEONIUM
Aeonium tabuliforme
p.35

CALICO HEARTS
Adromischus trigynus
p.33

GREEN PINWHEEL
Aeonium decorum
p.35

BLACK ROSE
*Aeonium arboreum
atropurpureum
'Zwartkop' pp.34–35*

CENTURY PLANT
Agave americana var.
mediopicta 'Alba'
pp.36–37

HEDGEHOG AGAVE
Agave stricta
p.37

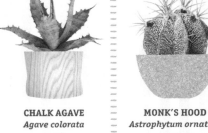

SPIDER ALOE
Aloe humilis
p.39

SILVER TORCH
Cleistocactus strausii
pp.44–45

CHALK AGAVE
Agave colorata
p.37

MONK'S HOOD
Astrophytum ornatum
pp.40–41

PERUVIAN APPLE
Cereus repandus
pp.42–43

MONKEY'S TAIL
*Cleistocactus winteri
colademono*
pp.46–47

TIGER ALOE
Aloe variegata
pp.38–39

GOAT'S HORN
*Astrophytum
capricorne*
p.41

FAIRY CASTLE
*Cereus monstrose
'Fairy Castle'*
p.43

SILVER CROWN
*Cotyledon orbiculata
var. oblonga (undulata)*
pp.48–49

ALOE VERA
p.39

BISHOP'S CAP
*Astrophytum
myriostigma*
p.41

SPIRAL CEREUS
*Cereus monstrose
'Spiralis'*
p.43

**COTYLEDON
AUSANA**
p.49

continued

COTYLEDON ORBICULATA OBLONGA
p.49

STRING OF BUTTONS
Crassula perforata
p.51

ECHEVERIA COLORATA
p.59

ECHINOCEREUS KNIPPELIANUS
p.63

ELEPHANT'S FOOT
Dioscorea elephantipes
pp.54–55

ROMEO WAX AGAVE
Echeveria agavoides
'Romeo'
p.59

ECHINOCEREUS VIERECKII MORRICALII
p.63

AIRPLANE PLANT
Crassula perfoliata var.
minor (falcata)
pp.50–51

RAT'S TAIL CACTUS
Disocactus
(formerly Aporocactus)
flagelliformis
pp.56–57

GOLDEN BARREL
Echinocactus grusonii
pp.60–61

PEANUT CACTUS
Echinopsis
chamaecereus
pp.64–65

JADE PLANT 'HUMMEL'S SUNSET'
Crassula ovata
'Hummel's Sunset' *p.51*

GHOST ECHEVERIA
Echeveria lilacina
pp.58–59

ECHINOCEREUS
Echinocereus subnermis
pp.62–63

ECHINOPSIS 'SPRING BLUSH'
p.66

**ECHINOPSIS
SUBDENUDATA 'TUFTY'**
p.67

**ECHINOPSIS
'TANGOED'**
p.67

ERIOSYCE SENILIS
Eriosyce (formerly
Neoporteria) senilis
pp.70–71

BASEBALL PLANT
Euphorbia obesa
p.75

**ECHINOPSIS
'SATURN'**
p.67

**ECHINOPSIS
'GALAXY'**
p.67

PERUVIAN OLD LADY
Epostoa melanostele
pp.72–73

WARTY TIGER JAWS
Faucaria tuberculosa
pp.76–77

FISHBONE CACTUS
*Epiphyllum
anguliger*
pp.68–69

SUZANNE'S SPURGE
Euphorbia suzannae
pp.74–75

BABY'S TOES
*Fenestraria
rhopalophylla* subsp.
aurantiaca
pp.78–79

PINE CONE PLANT
Euphorbia bupleurifolia
p.75

DEVIL'S TONGUE
Ferocactus latispinus
pp.82–83

continued

**FEROCACTUS
MACRODISCUS**
p. 83

CHIHUAHUA FLOWER
Graptopetalum bellum
(formerly *Tacitus*
bellus) *pp. 86–87*

**FEROCACTUS
HISTRIX**
p. 83

GYMNOCALYCIUM
Gymnocalycium bruchii
pp. 88–89

ZEBRA HAWORTHIA
Haworthia attenuata var. *clariperla*
pp. 90–91

BATE'S GASTERIA
Gasteria batesiana
pp. 84–85

**GYMNOCALYCIUM
CALOCHLORUM**
p. 89

PANDA PLANT
Kalanchoe tomentosa
pp. 92–93

FLAMING KATY
Kalanchoe blossfeldiana
p. 93

LAWYER'S TONGUE
Gasteria bicolor
p. 85

DWARF CHIN CACTUS
Gymnocalycium
baldianum
p. 89

DESERT SURPRISE
Kalanchoe humilis
p. 93

AGAVE CACTUS
Leuchtenbergia principis
pp. 94–95

LIVING STONES
Lithops marmorata
'Polepsky smaragd'
pp.96–97

MEXICAN PINCUSHION
Mammillaria magnimamma p.101

MATUCANA
Matucana madisoniorum
pp.102–03

ANGEL'S WINGS
Opuntia microdasys alba
pp.106–07

OLD LADY CACTUS
Mammillaria hahniana
pp.98–99

CARMEN'S PINCUSHION
Mammillaria carmenae
p.101

MATUCANA POLZII
p.103

COW'S TONGUE CACTUS
Opuntia engelmannii
p.107

MAMMILLARIA LONGIFLORA
p.100

FEATHER CACTUS
Mammillaria plumosa
p.101

MATUCANA KRAHNII
p.103

BEAVERTAIL CACTUS
Opuntia basilaris
p.107

LACE CACTUS
Mammillaria elongata
p.101

DWARF TURK'S CAP
Melocactus matanzanus
pp.104–05

STARFISH FLOWER
Orbea (formerly Stapelia)
variegata pp.110–11

continued

OREOCEREUS
Oreocereus leucotrichus
pp.112–13

GOLDEN POWDER PUFF
Parodia chrysacanthion
pp.116–17

SILVER BALL
Parodia scopa
p.119

CROWN CACTUS
Rebutia krainziana
pp.124–25

MOONSTONES
Pachyphytum oviferum
pp.114–15

**PARODIA
SUBTERRANEA**
p.117

**REBUTIA
HELIOSA**
p.126

**PACHYPHYTUM
COMPACTUM**
p.115

YELLOW TOWER
*Parodia (formerly
Notocactus) leninghausii*
pp.118–19

BLUE TORCH
Pilocereus pachycladus
pp.120–21

**REBUTIA
SENILIS**
p.127

**PACHYPHYTUM
HOOKERI**
p.115

BALL CACTUS
Parodia magnifica
p.119

PYGMAEOCEREUS
*Pygmaeocereus
bylesianus* pp.122–23

**REBUTIA
ALBIFLORA**
p.127

**REBUTIA
FLAVISTYLA**
p.127

CHRISTMAS CACTUS
*Schlumbergera
(formerly Zygocactus)
truncata*
pp.128–29

STRING OF BEADS
Senecio rowleyanus
pp.134–35

**SULCOREBUTIA
HERTUSII**
p.139

REBUTIA VIOLAFLORA
p.127

EASTER CACTUS
Hatiora gaertneri
p.129

BRAIN CACTUS
Stenocactus crispatus
pp.136–37

GLORY OF TEXAS
Thelocactus bicolor
pp.140–41

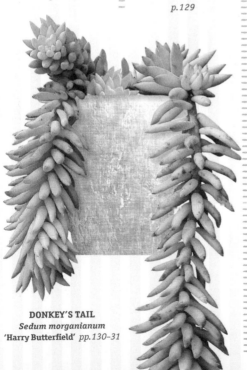

DONKEY'S TAIL
Sedum morganianum
'Harry Butterfield' *pp.130–31*

SULCOREBUTIA
Sulcorebutia rauschii
pp.138–39

**THELOCACTUS
BUEKII**
p.141

**SULCOREBUTIA
ARENACEA**
p.139

**THELOCACTUS
HEXAEDROPHORUS**
p.141

THE BASICS

MYTH-BUSTING

To help you better understand your cactus or succulent, and to make sure it thrives, it's useful to dispel some of the myths that surround these plants.

MYTH: CACTI ARE DIFFERENT FROM SUCCULENTS

TRUTH: All cacti belong to the group of plants called succulents, which are adapted to store water in their leaves, stems, and sometimes their roots. However, only cacti have round, cushion-like areas – called areoles – where spines can develop. In other succulents, there are no areoles although there may be spines.

Only cacti have areoles, from which spines grow

Blue torch (pp.120–21)

MYTH: THEY ARE ALL DESERT PLANTS

TRUTH: The ability to store water allows cacti and succulents to survive not only in hot, arid environments with limited rainfall (eg *Echinocereus*), but also on rocky outcrops (eg living stones), or as epiphytes, growing on the surface of other plants (eg Christmas cactus, which grows on trees in rainforests).

MYTH: THEY DON'T NEED WATERING

TRUTH: Cacti and succulents in the wild require seasonal rainfall in order to grow and produce flowers. See pp.22–23 for how to mimic this at home.

Echinocereus
(pp.62–63)

Living stones
(pp.96–97)

Christmas cactus
(pp.128–29)

MYTH: THEY ALL REQUIRE HOT, SUNNY CONDITIONS

TRUTH: Although many cacti and succulents need full sun during their growth period in order to thrive and flower, some require bright but indirect light (eg Chihuahua flower) to prevent their leaves becoming scorched. During their winter rest period, they need to be kept in a light place, but not below 5°C (41°F).

Chihuahua flower (pp.86–87)

MYTH: THEY'RE INDESTRUCTIBLE!

TRUTH: Cacti will only survive if cared for properly. This includes using the right, gritty, compost, not overwatering, and keeping them free from frost (eg dwarf Turk's cap).

Dwarf Turk's cap (pp.104–05)

MYTH: THEY GROW SLOWLY

TRUTH: Some cacti quickly produce a whole clump of new stems (eg crown cactus). Other fast-growing cacti include some trailing species that are suitable for growing in hanging pots.

Crown cactus (pp.124–25)

MYTH: THEY DON"T FLOWER EASILY

TRUTH: If they are given a winter resting period, and cared for correctly in spring and summer, most cacti will flower reliably. Many will produce spectacular blooms (eg glory of Texas), and some from an early age.

Glory of Texas produces "glorious" pink flowers

Glory of Texas (pp.140–41)

CHOOSE IT

There are a few things to consider when choosing your perfect cactus or succulent – and some important points to look out for when buying one.

THINGS TO CONSIDER

Think about the practical side of growing your cactus or succulent (eg where you'll grow it and how much time you have) and also its aesthetic appeal (eg flowers, leaf-shape, and overall size).

WHERE WILL I GROW IT?

You can grow cacti and succulents indoors or in a frost-free greenhouse. There are species suitable for small windowsills (eg *Gymnocalycium*, pp.88–89), hanging pots (eg rat's tail cactus, pp.56–57), full sunlight (eg baby's toes, pp.78–79), or bright but indirect light (eg golden powder puff, pp.116–17). You can also make a great showpiece for a wide windowsill by growing several cacti or succulents together in a large, shallow container.

Black rose
(pp.34–35)

String of buttons
(p.51)

Carmen's pincushion
(p.101)

HOW MUCH TIME CAN I SPARE?

Many cacti and succulents (eg airplane plant) are ideal for the beginner or anyone with a busy lifestyle. All they need is a sunny windowsill, watering every two weeks or so, and occasional feeding in the spring and summer.

Airplane plant
(pp.50–51)

DO I WANT A FAST-GROWING PLANT?

If patience is not your strong point, you could choose cacti or succulents that rapidly produce clusters of stems and that flower when they are relatively young (eg *Rebutia senilis*).

Rebutia senilis
(p.127)

WHAT TYPE OF FLOWERS DO I LIKE?

Some plants produce a stunning display (eg Easter cactus), some have scented blooms (eg string of beads, pp.134–35), and some are very exotic (eg glory of Texas, pp.140–41).

Easter cactus (p.129)

WHAT TYPE OF FOLIAGE DO I LIKE?

Many cacti and succulents are grown for their ornamental foliage, including those with mottled leaves (eg plover's eggs), striped leaves (eg tiger aloe, pp.38–39), or species that form intricate rosettes (eg ghost echeveria, pp.58–59).

Plover's eggs (pp.32–33)

BEFORE YOU BUY

If possible, buy your cactus or succulent from a nursery or garden centre, where it will have been properly cared for. Check that the compost is dry to the touch. If it is soggy, the cactus has been overwatered and may develop root rot. Avoid plants that are leggy or leaning towards the light, or ones with browning or yellowing of the leaves.

Healthy stem with no discoloration

Cactus is growing straight

Compost should be dry to the touch

Yellow tower (pp.118–19)

WHEN SHOULD I BUY IT?

Spring or summer is the best time to buy your cactus or succulent. If you are buying it in winter when it is cold, wrap it up before taking it home, to avoid exposing it to a sudden change in temperature.

cHOOSE A PuT

cacti and succulents can be grown in a wide range of containers, as long as they have at least one drainage hole to prevent root rot.

TYPES OF POT

Plastic, terracotta, or glazed ceramic pots and hanging containers are most suitable for cacti and succulents. Metal containers are not recommended because they change temperature too quickly.

Thelocactus buekii (p.141)

Elephant's foot (pp.54–55)

PLASTIC POT

Plastic pots are suitable for any surface, usually have several drainage holes, and are the cheapest option. As they are lightweight, they are not suitable for tall or top-heavy plants.

TERRACOTTA POT

Terracotta pots are considerably heavier than plastic pots, and their weight provides stability for plants that are tall or top-heavy. They are also porous, which helps to improve drainage and prevent waterlogging.

Monkey's tail
(pp.46–47)

You'll need a drainage tray to protect surfaces from water damage!

HANGING CONTAINERS

A range of hanging pots are available for growing trailing cacti indoors. Many have a built-in saucer to catch any drips during watering. Alternatively, a wire hanging basket lined with sphagnum moss can be used in a greenhouse.

Pygmaeocereus
(pp.122–23)

GLAZED-CERAMIC POT

These pots are available in a wide range of colours and designs, making them a popular decorative option. The heavy material also provides good stability. You may need to drill your own drainage holes.

SIZE OF POT

The size of the container will depend on the size of your plant. You will need to consider both diameter and depth.

DIAMETER Cacti don't need lots of space, so choose a pot that is about 2–3cm (1in) wider than your plant all round.

DEPTH Most cacti thrive in fairly shallow pots (often called "half pots"), but the container should not be less than 10cm (4in) in depth. Species with tuberous roots (eg some *Echinocereus*, pp.62–63) need a pot at least 15cm (6in) deep.

Small gap for growth

Pot should be slightly deeper than roots

Echinopsis 'tangoed'
(p.67)

PLANT & POSITION IT

Once you get your new plant home, you'll need to make sure it is potted correctly, and then find a suitable location that will meet its particular needs.

HOW TO PLANT IT

The soil provided with a shop-bought cactus or succulent often lacks the nutrients the plant needs to thrive. Therefore, you may want to repot your plant into new compost to keep it happy and healthy. Always protect your hands when handling prickly cacti (see p.24). If your plant is sold in an ornamental pot without drainage holes, you can double-pot with a slightly smaller plastic pot concealed on the inside. Be sure not to leave water standing in the ornamental pot after watering.

Echinopsis 'tangoed' (p.67)

Ensure the plastic pot fits snugly into the pot you want to use

CACTUS COMPOST

You can buy a proprietary cactus and succulent compost from garden centres, but it is easy – and more cost effective – to make your own. Just combine two parts of compost with one part of grit.

WHERE TO POSITION IT

The right spot for your cactus or succulent will depend on its specific needs in terms of light, temperature, and ventilation (see individual profiles). Your plant will also have different temperature requirements during its winter rest from those during its growth period.

LIGHT

Many cacti and succulents need a sunny situation, such as a south-facing windowsill or an unshaded greenhouse, but some prefer bright indirect or filtered light, such as an east- or west-facing windowsill or a shaded greenhouse, or even partial shade. Therefore, it is important to check the specific requirements of your plant.

Some plants may scorch in direct sunlight

Ghost echeveria (pp.58–59)

VENTILATION

In summer, it is important to provide good ventilation. On warm days, open the windows for cacti or succulents grown on a sill, or the vents and doors for plants grown in a greenhouse (automatic vents are recommended, as well as a wire mesh at the door opening to prevent wildlife entering).

Flaming Katy (p.93)

TEMPERATURE

→ Cacti and succulents do not like significant fluctuations in temperature, so avoid placing them near radiators or in draughts.

→ Never shut them behind curtains on cold nights.

→ During the plant's growth period in spring and summer, the daytime temperature should never be higher than 27–30°C (81–86°F). If you're growing your plant in a greenhouse, you may need to use shading if the temperature can't be controlled sufficiently by ventilation.

→ During winter, indoor cacti and succulents need cool night-time temperatures, but no lower than 5–10°C (41–50°F). Some cacti (eg, dwarf Turk's cap) are particularly sensitive to low temperatures. Plants in a greenhouse must be kept frost-free.

Dwarf Turk's cap (pp.104–05)

WATER & FEED IT

Cacti and succulents have a rather different watering and feeding regime to most other houseplants – timing is everything.

WHEN TO WATER

Cacti and succulents will thrive and flower if you mimic the seasonal rainfall pattern in their native habitat.

GROWTH PERIOD Water your cactus every two weeks or so during its growth period. In the northern hemisphere, this is from April until early September.

WINTER REST PERIOD From early September, gradually reduce watering, stopping altogether during the plant's winter rest period – from early November to the end of February. Gradually commence watering during March.

EXCEPTIONS TO THE RULE Winter-flowering cacti (eg Christmas cactus, pp.128–29) need to be watered every two weeks or so (and kept warm) until they finish flowering in late autumn or early winter.

HOW MUCH WATER?

Overwatering leads to root rot (see p.29), which is the main cause of death in cacti and succulents. However, by following a few simple steps you can prevent this from happening:

→ Make the compost moist but not wet, and allow all excess water to drain away after each watering.

→ Allow the compost to become almost dry between waterings.

→ Check the moisture level of the compost by sliding a label or knife blade down the inside of the pot – if it comes out clean, the soil is dry.

→ Remember that compost in plastic and glazed ceramic containers retains moisture for longer than it does in terracotta pots, so you will need to water slightly less frequently.

Slide a label or knife blade into the compost

If it comes out clean, the soil is dry

Parodia subterranea (p.117)

HOW TO WATER

Most plants can be watered from above. However, if your cactus has hairy leaves (eg panda plant), or its leaves and stems cover the compost, water it from below to avoid splashing them. If possible, use rainwater (leave a bucket outside to collect it), as some cacti are sensitive to the minerals in tap water. Tepid water is best.

FROM ABOVE
Use a watering can with a long, thin spout to reach the compost easily. Water the compost evenly around the base of the plant.

Echinocereus (pp.62–63)

FROM BELOW
Stand the pot in a saucer of water for around 30 minutes. Then drain any excess water from the saucer.

Water is absorbed from below

Panda plant (pp.92–93)

"Stop watering your plant altogether during its winter rest period and only resume in spring."

FEEDING

Like all plants, cacti and succulents need food in order to thrive. Add a high-potash feed, such as liquid tomato fertilizer, to the watering can two or three times during the growth period (from April to September). Be sure to follow the manufacturer's instructions and don't be tempted to add extra – overfeeding can damage the plant.

Add liquid feed when watering

Moonstones (pp.114–15)

REPOT IT

When your plant has become "pot bound" and its roots have filled the container, you will need to repot it. This is also a good time to replenish its compost.

WHEN TO REPOT

After about two to four years, depending on how fast the particular species grows, your plant will have filled its pot.

→ First, check whether any roots are growing through the drainage holes at the base of the container. This is a sure sign that a larger pot is needed.
→ If no roots are visible externally, carefully remove the rootball and check whether the roots are curling round the edge of the compost. This is another clue that the plant is "pot bound".
→ The best time for repotting is in early spring, at the end of the plant's winter rest period.

Roots coming out of the bottom of the pot

Brain cactus (p.136)

HANDLING CACTI
Always wear gloves when handling spiny cacti. In some species (eg devil's tongue, pp.82–83) the spines are sharp enough to penetrate gloves, so for extra protection wrap a cloth or a strip of crumpled newspaper around the plant. An oven glove can be very useful when handling large, tall, or heavy plants.

"After repotting your plant, continue to care for it as normal."

HOW TO REPOT

To repot your cactus or succulent you only
need to follow a few simple steps.

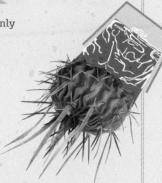

*Layer of
gravel*

1 Never water your plant
before repotting it.
Choose a clean pot that is
only slightly larger than the
present one, as cacti and
succulents prefer a snug fit.

2 Put a shallow layer of gravel
in the bottom of the new
pot, and cover this with a layer
of fresh, dry compost. Either
use a premade cactus compost,
or make your own (see p.20).

3 Gently slide your
cactus out of its pot
and tease out any roots
that are coiling round
the rootball. Be careful
not to damage them.

*Leave
1–2cm
(1in) at
top of pot*

4 Place the cactus in
its new container, no
deeper than it was in the
original pot.

5 Carefully add more dry compost
around the rootball, firming it
in gently. Leave space between the
surface of the compost and pot.

6 Wait for at least two
weeks after repotting
before watering your
cactus or succulent.

SHARE IT

Depending on the type of cactus or succulent you want to share, you can propagate it by taking leaf or stem cuttings, dividing offsets, or sowing seed.

LEAF CUTTINGS

You can take leaf cuttings from some succulents in spring or early summer a week or so after watering.

1 Remove a healthy leaf by easing it off gently from side to side from the parent plant. It must come away with the base intact.

Ghost echeveria (pp.58–59)

2 Allow the cutting to dry for a few days. Then insert its base in compost made of one part fine peat substitute to one part gritty sand, in a small pot.

3 When you can see a new plantlet growing at the base of the cutting, pot it up in dry compost, watering after a week or two.

New growth

STEM CUTTINGS

Take stem cuttings in early spring, a week or so after watering. Cut a healthy stem close to its base with a sharp knife. Trim the cutting just below a leaf joint, leave to dry for a week, and then lay on compost. Water once roots appear.

STEM SECTIONS Use this method for cacti that have jointed sections or a number of stems. Remove a stem by cutting across the joint with a sharp knife. Allow the cuttings to dry for a week or so, and then insert them in compost in the same way as stem cuttings.

Cut across joint

Angel's wings (pp.106–07)

DIVIDING CLUMP-FORMING OFFSETS

You can divide and take cuttings from the clump-forming offsets of clustering cacti in spring.

Crown cactus (pp.124–25)

Cut offset from parent

Peat and sand mix

1 Gently scrape away the top layer of compost to expose the base of the offsets (young plants).

2 Carefully sever one or more of the offsets where they join the parent plant.

3 Allow them to dry for a week or so and then insert them in dry compost. Water when roots appear.

SOWING SEED

Sowing seed is a good way to grow a particular species that you can't otherwise find for sale. Sow seed in early spring.

Sprinkle seeds on surface

New seedlings

Living stones (pp.96–97)

1 Put a shallow layer of gravel, mixed with a little charcoal, in the bottom of a clean pot. Fill with fresh seed compost, firm it lightly, and cover the surface with a thin layer of fine grit.

2 Sprinkle the seeds evenly over the gritty surface. Water from below in a saucer, tipping away any remaining water after half an hour.

3 Put the pot in a plastic bag in a warm place – 21°C (70°F) is ideal – in good light but not direct sunlight. Remove the bag when the seedlings appear. Keep out of direct sunlight for the first year.

PESTS & DISEASES

Although cacti and succulents are fairly hardy plants, they can be visited by a few unwelcome guests. Here are some common problems and how to deal with them.

PREVENTING PESTS

You can help prevent pests by keeping your plant healthy during its growing period. Use fresh compost to avoid transferring pests from other plants, and remove any fallen leaves. When using insecticides, always follow the manufacturer's instructions. If several plants in a greenhouse have the same pest, try a biological control instead. These products work by using a natural predator of the pest to destroy it (use in summer as some will not tolerate low temperatures).

MEALYBUGS

These slow-moving, wingless insects produce a fluffy, white substance on the leaves and stems. Root mealybugs cause damage to roots.

☀ TREAT IT

Remove small infestations of leaves and stems by dabbing them with a cotton bud soaked in methylated spirits, followed quickly by an insecticidal spray (wear a mask for this). Severe infestations stunt the plant's growth, so use an insecticide or a biological control in summer and remove all traces of the woolly material.

RED SPIDER MITES

This yellow-orange pest can cause a lot of damage. Look out for mottled and yellowing leaves, premature leaf fall, and a fine webbing over the plant.

☀ TREAT IT

This minute pest spreads rapidly in dry, poorly ventilated conditions, so deter it by opening the windows in warm weather. Check for mites with a powerful magnifying glass, and treat affected plants with an insecticide or a biological control in summer.

Area of attack

Peanut cactus
(pp.64–65)

"Use fresh compost to avoid transferring pests between plants."

FUNGUS GNATS

Also known as sciarid flies, these tiny insects fly around the plant. The flies are annoying but not harmful. However, their larvae can attack the roots of young plants.

❤ TREAT IT

Use a yellow sticky trap to catch the adult flies. Always remove dead leaves and flowers from the compost surface. Water thoroughly with an insecticide to kill the larvae, and repeat when gnats are seen.

Sticky trap

Matucana (pp.102–03)

SCALE INSECTS

These limpet-like insects appear as small, brown, raised areas on stems and the undersides of leaves. If not controlled, they will weaken affected plants.

❤ TREAT IT

Rub off the scale, apply methylated spirits with a cotton bud, then immediately spray the affected areas with insecticide.

Scale insects attached to a leaf ·········

Fishbone cactus (pp.68–69)

DISEASES

The best defence against fungal diseases is to avoid overwatering (see p.22).

ROOT ROT

This is a fungal disease of the roots that is caused by waterlogging. Affected roots are soft and dark, and the disease will eventually cause the collapse of the plant.

☀ TREAT IT

Remove the compost to check the roots. Trim off any diseased roots, and repot the plant in fresh compost in a new, clean pot. Treat it with a fungicide after two or three weeks.

PRICKLY
PROFILES

PLOVER'S EGGS

Adromischus cooperi

This succulent, one of nearly 30 species in the genus, is easy to grow. Its attractively patterned leaves make it a perfect windowsill decoration.

:::

VITAL STATISTICS

- **HOW IT GROWS** This slow-growing dwarf succulent branches freely to form a small cluster of stems.

HANDLE WITH CARE
This plant should be handled gently as the leaves are very easily knocked off.

- **ANATOMY** The thick, fleshy, grey-green leaves of this species have wavy tips and are up to 5cm (2in) long. Their upper surface is green and mottled with purple spots, resembling the pattern on a plover's egg – hence the plant's common name.

- **SIZE** This plant grows up to 10cm (4in) in height and 15cm (6in) across. It develops new leaves each year in spring and summer to reach this maximum size.

Indoors: 10cm (4in)

WATER ME

Water me every two weeks or so in spring and summer, when my compost is nearly dry. Don't water me from mid-autumn to early spring.

POSITION ME

I need bright sunlight to produce vivid leaf colours, so put me on a south-facing windowsill (but don't shut me behind curtains on cold nights).

HELP ME FLOWER

If you care for me well, I will produce small, reddish, tubular flowers on tall stems in midsummer. My flowers are quite modest in comparison with my leaves.

SHARE ME

Remove individual leaves with the base intact, and place them on dry compost. When roots appear, insert them into the compost, watering about a week later.

CALICO HEARTS
Adromischus trigynus
This species grows up to 15cm (6in) tall, and has convex leaves with striking purple mottling. It has similar care needs to its smaller relative.

I come from South Africa.

REPOT ME

Repot me in early spring after two or three years, when my roots have filled the pot. Use dry compost in a slightly bigger pot. Don't water me for at least two weeks afterwards.

FEED ME

Add a high-potash fertilizer to my water two or three times in spring and summer.

BLACK ROSE

Aeonium arboreum atropurpureum 'Zwartkop'

This branching, tree-like succulent is a cultivar (cultivated variety) with broader leaves than others of this species.

VITAL STATISTICS

● **HOW IT GROWS** Black rose is a relatively tall, branching plant. The leaves form at the tips of the branches.

EXTRA SUPPORT
As the plant grows, you may need to support it with a bamboo stick. Push the stick into the soil near the central stem, then tie loosely.

● **ANATOMY** The black rose succulent gets its common name from the colour and shape of its leaves, which form flower-like rosettes that are dark purple or almost black. It produces clusters of striking yellow flowers on the mature branches.

● **SIZE** Black rose will grow quite quickly, producing a cluster of branches 1m (3ft) or more in height after about two to five years.

Indoors: 1m (3ft)

WATER ME
Treat me like most succulents, watering me only during the spring and summer, and when my soil is nearly dry (about every two weeks).

POSITION ME
I thrive on direct sunlight, which brings out the best colouring of my leaves and prevents thin, lanky growth.

HELP ME FLOWER
I prefer subtropical conditions. In cooler climates, I will have the best chance of flowering if you place me in full sun.

SHARE ME
Take cuttings in spring or summer, laying them on fresh, dry compost. When new roots appear, plant them carefully, supporting each cutting with a stick.

REPOT ME
Repot me in early spring after two or three years, when my roots will have filled the pot. Use dry compost and a slightly bigger pot.

FEED ME
Add a high-potash fertilizer to my water two or three times in spring and summer.

I come from the Canary Islands.

MEET THE RELATIVES

FLAT-TOPPED AEONIUM
Aeonium tabuliforme
Forming a flat disc of green leaves, this species of Aeonium also produces clusters of yellow flowers, which erupt in the centre of the plant.

GREEN PINWHEEL
Aeonium decorum
This species, also from the Aeonium genus, is a shrubby, branching plant with attractive leaf colouring.

CENTURY PLANT

Agave americana var. *mediopicta* 'Alba'

This small variety of the popular century plant comes from a genus with nearly 200 species. Most members of the genus are too large for windowsill growing.

VITAL STATISTICS

● **HOW IT GROWS** This plants grows long leaves in a rosette formation. Each leaf has a central, cream-coloured stripe.

● **ANATOMY** Agaves are a very tough group of succulents, with sharp, pointy leaves and jagged teeth. These plants rarely attract pests and can tolerate low temperatures. They can produce flowers, but only at the very end of the plant's life.

UNIQUE MARKINGS
There are many variegated agave species, all with different patterns of attractive stripes.

● **SIZE** This particular agave is the smallest of the species. At its maximum height, it will need a pot no bigger than 40–50cm (16–20in) in diameter.

Indoors: 40–50cm (16–20in)

WATER ME
Water me every two weeks or so in spring and summer, when my soil is nearly dry. Don't water me from mid-autumn to spring.

POSITION ME
I need full sunshine to grow properly, so a windowsill with lots of light is ideal.

SHARE ME

You can remove my offset rosettes with a sharp knife, leaving them to dry for a couple of weeks before repotting. The offsets will have usually formed their own roots, but if not, you can dust them with hormone rooting powder to encourage growth.

REPOT ME

My roots will have filled my pot within two or three years. Re-home me in early spring a week or two before you start watering again.

I come from Mexico and the USA.

FEED ME

Add a high-potash fertilizer to my water two or three times in the growing period (spring and summer).

HEDGEHOG AGAVE
Agave stricta
This member of the genus has multiple thin, spiky leaves that can grow up to 40cm (16in) long.

MESCAL CENIZA
Agave colorata
This larger species has wide, blue-tinged leaves that are lined with dark brown teeth. It can grow up to 1m (3ft) tall.

TIGER ALOE

Aloe variegata

Named after its stripy leaf pattern (it's also known as partridge-breasted aloe for the same reason), this member of the huge aloe genus is a popular choice.

VITAL STATISTICS

● **HOW IT GROWS** *Aloe variegata* grows clusters of triangular, stripy leaves in a rosette formation.

MISTAKEN IDENTITY
It doesn't have the medicinal properties of its relative *Aloe vera*, so never eat it or try to use it for healing purposes!

● **ANATOMY** The leaves of this plant culminate in firm, sharp points, giving it a striking appearance and providing protection in the wild. If you look closely, you can see little white teeth lining the edges of each leaf.

● **SIZE** This species is one of the smallest aloes, and very slow growing. It takes about eight years to make a full-sized rosette. As a houseplant, it can reach a maximum height and spread of 25cm (10in).

Indoors: 25cm (10in)

WATER ME
Water me every two weeks or so in the spring and summer, when my soil is nearly dry. Don't water me from mid-autumn to spring.

POSITION ME
I need sunshine to grow properly, so a sunny windowsill or greenhouse kept above 4°C (40°F) is ideal. Indoors, don't shut me behind curtains on cold nights!

REPOT ME

My roots will fill my pot within two or three years. Repot me in early spring into a slightly bigger pot. Use dry compost and don't water me for two weeks afterwards.

HELP ME FLOWER

Keep me dry and cool in winter to encourage flowering. Reddish-pink flowers appear on a stem that grows from the middle of the rosette when I have produced about a dozen leaves.

FEED ME

Add a high-potash fertilizer to my water two or three times in the growing period (spring and summer).

SHARE ME

You can gently remove my offset rosettes when repotting. They will usually have formed roots, but if not, you can dust them with hormone rooting powder to encourage growth.

I come from South Africa and Namibia.

MEET THE RELATIVES

ALOE VERA
This popular plant has spiky, fleshy leaves. The sap is used to soothe burns and skin irritation.

SPIDER ALOE
Aloe humilis
This small member of the genus has distinctive leaves covered in irregularly spaced bumps. It produces bright red-orange flowers.

MONK'S HOOD

Astrophytum ornatum

This cactus is the largest member of a genus containing only six species. It is fairly easy to grow, but requires a wide windowsill when it gets big.

VITAL STATISTICS

● **HOW IT GROWS** This plant starts as a young globular plant and eventually becomes thick and columnar.

TAKE CARE
This plant's protective spines are sharp enough to penetrate gloves. For extra protection, wrap a cloth around it when repotting.

● **ANATOMY** Monk's hood has strong yellowish spines that run down the length of its ribs. In the wild, these help protect the plant from being eaten. The surface of the plant has distinct white woolly flecks.

● **SIZE** This species takes about 10 years to grow 30cm (12in) tall and 15–20cm (6–8in) wide. Indoors, it can eventually reach 1m (3ft) in height. In the wild, ancient plants have even been recorded at heights of 3m (10ft)!

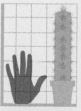

Indoors: 30cm (12in)

WATER ME
Water me every two weeks or so in the spring and summer, when my soil is nearly dry. Don't water me from mid-autumn to spring.

POSITION ME
I need a sunny position to thrive, like all members of my genus. Don't expose me to temperatures below 5°C (41°F).

HELP ME FLOWER

Full exposure to sunlight helps me flower. My flowers are yellow or, more rarely, white and grow at my crown after I reach about 10cm (4in) in height – or earlier if you're lucky!

SHARE ME

You might have to keep me to yourself! This genus doesn't cluster, so I can only be propagated by growing from seeds (see p.27). These are produced by cross-pollinating two plants.

I come from Mexico.

FEED ME

Add a high-potash fertilizer to my water two or three times in the growing period (spring and summer).

GOAT'S HORN
Astrophytum capricorne
This plant has long, curved spines and produces yellow flowers with a red centre. It requires the same care as its larger relative.

REPOT ME

Repot me in early spring into a slightly bigger pot. Use dry compost and don't water me for about two weeks afterwards.

BISHOP'S CAP
Astrophytum myriostigma
This spineless member of the genus usually has five ribs. It only needs to reach about 5–8cm (2–3in) in height to flower.

PERUVIAN APPLE

Cereus repandus

In the wild, this cactus forms a branching, tree-like structure up to 12m (40ft) in height. Indoors it is smaller, but still makes for a tall houseplant.

VITAL STATISTICS

● **HOW IT GROWS** This columnar cactus forms branches as it matures.

HELPING HAND

As this cactus grows taller, you may need help to lift and support it when repotting. Wrap the prickly stems in a soft cloth.

● **ANATOMY** The Peruvian apple cactus has green or grey-green stems with 7–12 spined ribs. If exposed to temperatures below 7°C (45°F), brown marks may appear on the stem and the plant may collapse.

● **SIZE** This cactus grows fairly quickly. From a seedling plant of about 15cm (6in), it will reach a height of approximately 45cm (18in) after four to six years, and will continue to grow taller.

Indoors: 45cm (18in)

WATER ME

Water me every two weeks or so in spring and summer, when my soil is nearly dry. Don't water me from mid-autumn to spring.

POSITION ME

Place me on a sunny windowsill or in a greenhouse. I need sunshine and a minimum temperature of 7°C (45°F) to stay happy.

HELP ME FLOWER

Keep me healthy and growing steadily to encourage my flowers. These open at night when I reach at least 40cm (16in) in height. Usually several white flowers tinged pink or green appear for a week or two.

SHARE ME

If or when I start to branch, these can be used as cuttings in early summer when about 15cm (6in) long. Allow the cut end to dry, then place on compost with a layer of sand. Only start to water once roots have formed.

REPOT ME

Move me in early spring into a slightly bigger pot. Choose a heavy container as I may topple as I grow taller. Use dry compost and don't water me for at least two weeks.

FEED ME

Add a high-potash fertilizer to my water two or three times in the growing period (spring and summer).

I come from Venezuela and the Antilles.

MEET THE RELATIVES

FAIRY CASTLE
Cereus monstrose
'Fairy Castle'
This columnar cactus is named after its collection of small, turret-like stems. Its flowers are rare.

SPIRAL CEREUS
Cereus monstrose
'Spiralis'
This mutant cereus plant grows in a tight spiral shape. Its unusual appearance makes it a very popular houseplant.

SILVER TORCH

Cleistocactus strausii

This columnar cactus looks impressive, but is small enough to be kept indoors. It is named after its long, thin shape and silvery spines.

VITAL STATISTICS

● **HOW IT GROWS** Silver torch takes several years to grow from a tiny seedling into a tall, columnar plant.

TIMBER!
Silver torch has a tendency to lean towards the light and may even topple over. To prevent this, rotate the pot a little bit every few weeks.

● **ANATOMY** The green stem of this cactus is densely covered with fine, needle-like white spines. It tends to stay solitary until flowering size. The tip of the column is prone to dying back if not cared for properly.

● **SIZE** It takes about five years for a single seedling to reach a height when it can flower – generally about 50–60cm (20–24in), although the plant may flower earlier in full sun. At this point, fresh shoots may also appear at the base.

Indoors: 50–60cm
(20–24in)

WATER ME
Only water me in the spring and summer months. Check my soil is nearly dry before watering (every two weeks or so). I don't get thirsty from mid-autumn to spring.

POSITION ME
Full exposure to sunlight helps me grow properly and produce healthy spines. A sunny windowsill or greenhouse is ideal.

SHARE ME

Remove offsets from my stem when they are 10cm (4in) tall. Leave these to dry for about a week before placing on fresh compost and sand. Help the little ones stand up by loosely tying them to a stick.

REPOT ME

Repot me in early spring into a slightly bigger pot. Use dry compost and don't water me for about two weeks afterwards. Wrap soft material around my stem when moving me – so you don't damage my spines or hurt your hands.

HELP ME FLOWER

Keep me happy to help me reach a flowering height of 50–60cm (20–24in). My tubular flowers flare at the tips and form on the top side of my column. Usually, several flowers open for a week or two in summer.

I come from South America.

FEED ME

Add a high-potash fertilizer to my water two or three times in the summer to ensure continual growth.

MONKEY'S TAIL

Cleistocactus winteri colademono

Only recently discovered but already a very popular plant, monkey's tail is one of a few hanging species in the genus. It is named after its long furry "tails".

VITAL STATISTICS

● **HOW IT GROWS** This plant steadily produces new, upright stems from the base. These begin to hang as they grow.

FURRY FACT

The "tails" really are soft to touch! Just make sure you stroke them downwards, in the direction of spine growth.

● **ANATOMY** Monkey's tail is covered in long, white, hair-like spines that get denser with age. In the wild it trails over rocks and trees, at home it is best suited to a hanging pot. The stem tips are prone to dying back if the plant is not cared for properly.

● **SIZE** The maximum size of monkey's tail is not known as it has only recently become widely available as a houseplant, but stems have been recorded at nearly 1m (3ft). It is estimated they could reach 2m (6ft) in length.

Indoors: 1m (3ft)

WATER ME

Water me every two weeks or so in the spring and summer, when my soil is nearly dry. Don't water me from mid-autumn to spring.

POSITION ME

I need a sunny spot to grow happily. Rotate my pot a little bit each month to ensure each of my stems gets enough sunlight.

FEED ME

Include a high-potash fertilizer in my water two or three times during spring and summer.

HELP ME FLOWER

Keep me happy and healthy to encourage my bright red, tubular flowers. I produce these towards the tips of my hanging stems once they reach about 15cm (6in) in length.

REPOT ME

Repot me in early spring into a slightly bigger pot with dry compost. When moving me, wrap me in a soft material to protect my spines. Don't water me for two weeks afterwards.

SHARE ME

Cut off one of my sprouting stems in early summer when it is 8–10cm (3–4in) long. Leave it to dry for a week, then place on fresh compost with a layer of sand to encourage root growth. This can then be potted and watered.

I come from Bolivia.

SILVER CROWN

Cotyledon orbiculata var. oblonga (undulata)

This popular, sculptural succulent has interesting crinkle-edged leaves. It makes a striking feature plant all year but especially when it flowers in summer.

IIIIIIIIIIIIIIIIIIIIIIIIIIIIIIIIIIIIIIIIIIIIIIIIIIIIIIIIIIIIIIIIIIIIIIIIIIIIII

VITAL STATISTICS

● **HOW IT GROWS** This succulent is a gradually branching, shrubby plant that becomes as tall as it is wide.

KEEP IN CHECK
As it branches, this succulent may outgrow your windowsill. Cut off some branches to keep it within bounds.

● **ANATOMY** Silver crown comprises flat, grey-green leaves like paddles or scallop shells that have a powdery, waxy coating. It produces a long stem of elegant flowers in summer, then fruits if it is pollinated – although this rarely happens indoors.

● **SIZE** When fully grown – after about five years – its height and spread will be 60cm (24in). Flowers add a further 15cm (6in). Silver crown needs good light to maintain its compact, branching structure – and not become "leggy".

Indoors: 60cm (24in)

WATER ME
Water me in spring and summer every two weeks or when my compost is nearly dry. Stop from mid-autumn to spring.

POSITION ME
I need a sunny windowsill or a lightly shaded but frost-free greenhouse or frame.

SHARE ME

Take cuttings just below the bottom leaves on one of my branches. Place them on compost with a layer of sand. Water when roots appear, and insert them into the compost.

HELP ME FLOWER

I produce tubular, coral-red flowers every year on an erect flower stem.

Petals flare at the tip as they open

MEET THE RELATIVES

COTYLEDON AUSANA
There are many different forms of C. orbiculata, *such as this example (formerly known as C. undulata), which has similar but more disc-shaped leaves.*

I come from South Africa.

REPOT ME

Repot me every two or three years in early spring when my roots have filled the pot. Choose a slightly larger pot and don't water me for two weeks afterwards.

FEED ME

Feed me with a high-potash fertilizer two or three times in spring and summer.

COTYLEDON ORBICULATA OBLONGA
This variable species also has grey-green, oval-shaped leaves, although its flowers are orange and bell-shaped. It may reach 0.5–1m (20–40in) after about ten years.

AIRPLANE PLANT

Crassula perfoliata var. minor (falcata)

As well as being easy to grow, this plant has attractive grey-green leaves and clusters of tiny, star-shaped flowers, making it a perfect windowsill decoration.

VITAL STATISTICS

● **HOW IT GROWS** This bushy, evergreen succulent gradually increases in size by producing side shoots.

SIZE MATTERS

If it's getting too large for your windowsill, simply trim its side shoots. Root the trimmings to make new plants.

● **ANATOMY** The thick, sickle-shaped leaves, which are up to 10cm (4in) long, are produced in overlapping pairs. This propeller-like arrangement has inspired its common names, which include airplane plant and propeller plant.

● **SIZE** In the wild, this plant can grow to 1m (3ft) in height and spread. Even when grown as a houseplant, it can still reach a height of 60cm (24in), with a spread of up to 75cm (30in).

Indoors: 60cm (24in)

WATER ME

Water me every two weeks or so in the spring and summer, when my compost is nearly dry. Don't water me from mid-autumn to spring.

SHARE ME

Take side shoots as cuttings and place them on fresh compost. When roots appear, insert them into the compost to grow on.

POSITION ME

I am equally happy indoors on a sunny windowsill or in a lightly shaded greenhouse kept above 5°C (41°F).

HELP ME FLOWER

Care for me well and I'll flower in late summer when I'm a few years old. My blooms will last for nearly a month, and their colour will be most vivid if you grow me in bright light.

REPOT ME

Repot me in early spring after two or three years, when my roots have filled the pot. Use dry compost in a slightly bigger pot and don't water me for at least two weeks afterwards.

I come from South Africa.

FEED ME

Add a high-potash fertilizer to my water two or three times during spring and summer.

MEET THE RELATIVES

JADE PLANT 'HUMMEL'S SUNSET'
***Crassula ovata* 'Hummel's Sunset'**
This shrubby species has glossy leaves tinged with red. It requires the same care as its relative.

STRING OF BUTTONS
Crassula perforata
This small, shrubby succulent has short, grey-green leaves with pink margins, and produces tiny, white, star-shaped flowers. It has similar care needs to the airplane plant.

TOP FIVE...
BIG SHOWSTOPPERS

Some cacti and succulents are so striking that they deserve to be shown off. Here are some big, impressive species that will make a statement in your home.

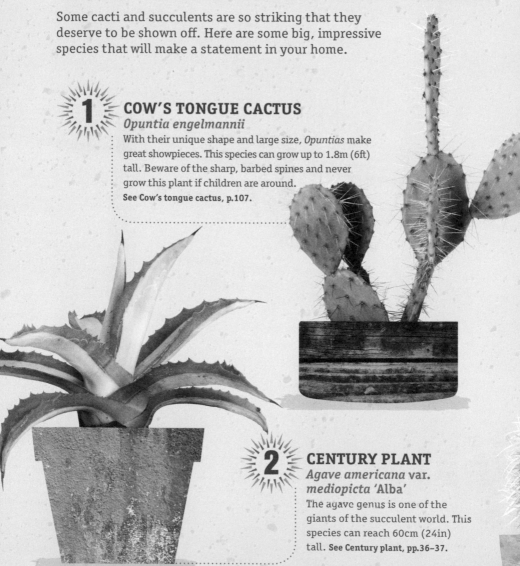

1

COW'S TONGUE CACTUS
Opuntia engelmannii

With their unique shape and large size, *Opuntias* make great showpieces. This species can grow up to 1.8m (6ft) tall. Beware of the sharp, barbed spines and never grow this plant if children are around.
See Cow's tongue cactus, p.107.

2

CENTURY PLANT
Agave americana var. *mediopicta* 'Alba'

The agave genus is one of the giants of the succulent world. This species can reach 60cm (24in) tall. **See Century plant, pp.36–37.**

3 OREOCEREUS
Oreocereus leucotrichus
The stems of this woolly, clustering cactus can eventually reach 1–2m (3–6ft) in height. It makes an attractive centrepiece in a large room.

See *Oreocereus*, pp.112–13.

4 PERUVIAN APPLE
Cereus repandus
A huge, branching species in the wild, this cactus can also reach an impressive height in your home. Within four to six years it will grow to about 45cm (18in) tall.

See Peruvian apple, pp.42–43.

5 GOLDEN BARREL
Echinocactus grusonii
This popular cactus can grow up to 70cm (28in) across. Rotate it regularly to prevent it distorting from uneven sun exposure.

See Golden barrel, pp.60–61.

ELEPHANT'S FOOT

Dioscorea elephantipes

This slow-growing climbing succulent will live for up to 70 years if well cared for. With its above-ground tuber, it is an ideal plant for a container.

llllllllllllllllllllllllllllllllllllllllllllllllllllllllllllllllllll

VITAL STATISTICS

● **HOW IT GROWS** Vine-like stems grow from the top of the tuber each year, dying back at the end of the growing season.

TAKE CARE!
The tuber of this plant contains toxic compounds, so keep it out of reach of children and pets.

● **ANATOMY** This plant is named after its partially buried woody tuber, which can grow to a diameter of 1m (3ft). As the plant matures, the tuber takes on a fissured appearance and has been said to resemble an elephant's foot.

● **SIZE** The vine-like stem can reach a height and spread of 1m (3ft) or more, and will need a support such as a sturdy cane or trellis to twine around.

Indoors: 1m (3ft)

WATER ME
Water me every two weeks or so in the spring and summer, when my compost is nearly dry. Don't water me from mid-autumn to spring.

POSITION ME
To thrive, I need to be in a fairly sunny position, such as on a south-east- or south-west-facing windowsill.

SHARE ME

You may need to keep me to myself as I can only be grown from seeds (see p.27). These are produced by cross-pollinating two plants.

HELP ME FLOWER

If you care for me well, I will produce tiny yellow flowers among the leaves of my top-growth when I'm a few years old.

FEED ME

Add a high-potash fertilizer to my water two or three times during spring and summer.

REPOT ME

This is best done in early spring, at the end of my winter rest. Repot me in dry compost in a slightly bigger pot, and don't water me for at least two weeks afterwards.

I come from South Africa.

RAT'S TAIL CACTUS

Disocactus (formerly Aporocactus) flagelliformis

This is a very popular, thin-stemmed tree cactus, best grown in a hanging pot. The flowering "rat's tail" stems can grow to about 1m (3ft) in length.

VITAL STATISTICS

● **HOW IT GROWS** The rat's tail is a trailing cactus, growing long, thin stems from the top of the plant.

DRIP, DRIP, DRIP!
If you grow the plant indoors, use a hanging pot with a built-in saucer to prevent drips.

● **ANATOMY** This plant often grows on the shady side of trees, or sprawling over rocks. It likes a compost comprising two parts peat or coir to one part bark chippings to imitate its natural habitat. The stems can wither if they get too dry.

● **SIZE** The hanging stems of this plant can grow to 1m (3ft) or more in length if regularly potted on. By the time they get this long, younger shoots will have started appearing from the top.

Indoors: 1m (3ft)

WATER ME
Water me regularly in spring and summer, easing off in early autumn. Keep me dry between late autumn and the end of winter.

POSITION ME
I need dappled sunlight to thrive, so a sunny spot with partial shade is perfect. My home should be a hanging pot to allow me to trail.

HELP ME FLOWER

I need a combination of light and shade to flower, which I do in summer. Once my stems have reached about 20cm (8in), they should produce deep pink flowers.

SHARE ME

Cut off one of my stems when several have formed, and divide into pieces about 7cm (3in) long. Lay these on dry compost with a thin top layer of sand to encourage root growth.

FEED ME

Add a high-potash fertilizer to my water two or three times during the spring and summer months.

REPOT ME

Move me into a slightly larger hanging pot in early spring every three or four years (you'll need help to do this). Wrap me in a soft cloth to protect me from damage and to prevent injury to you or your helper. Use dry compost and wait a week or two before watering.

I come from Mexico.

GHOST ECHEVERIA

Echeveria lilacina

This succulent forms a rosette of lilac-grey leaves. It is easy to grow and makes an attractive feature, either on its own or as part of a collection of Echeverias.

VITAL STATISTICS

● **HOW IT GROWS** This plant usually stays solitary (although many other species will go on to form clusters of rosettes).

SUN PROTECTION
Don't expose this plant to too much direct sunlight in early spring, otherwise its leaves may become scorched.

● **ANATOMY** The pointed, spoon-shaped leaves have a ghostly "bloom". This is because they are covered with a layer of farina – a powdery substance that helps protect the plant from strong sunlight. This will rub off if the plant is not handled carefully.

● **SIZE** The leaves of this species are produced in a symmetrical arrangement to form a rosette that can eventually reach a diameter of 13–25cm (5–10in). The flower stems grow to a height of up to 15cm (6in).

Indoors: 15cm (6in)

WATER ME
Water me every two weeks or so in spring and summer, when my compost is nearly dry. Don't water me from mid-autumn to early spring.

POSITION ME
I need some sunlight, but not too much. I am happy on a south-east- or south-west-facing windowsill (but don't shut me behind curtains on cold nights).

HELP ME FLOWER

Follow my care advice and, in spring, I will produce slender flower stems bearing small, tubular flowers.

SHARE ME

Remove a whole leaf with the base intact, and place it on dry, fresh compost. Roots will develop first, followed by a tiny, new rosette.

MEET THE RELATIVES

ECHEVERIA COLORATA
This species produces rosettes up to 20cm (8in) in diameter, consisting of finely pointed, pale blue leaves that are tipped with red. It requires the same care as its relative.

I come from Mexico.

FEED ME

Add a high-potash fertilizer to my water two or three times during spring and summer.

REPOT ME

Repot me after two or three years, when my roots have filled the pot. Use dry compost in a slightly bigger pot.

ROMEO WAX AGAVE
Echeveria agavoides **'Romeo'**
This species has greyish-purple spiny leaves and produces a cluster of rosettes up to 30cm (12in) across. It has similar care needs to its relative.

GOLDEN BARREL

Echinocactus grusonii

One of the most popular cacti worldwide, golden barrel is now rare in the wild. It is named after its shape and colour, and is also known as mother-in-law's cushion!

|||||||||||||||||||||||||||||||||||||||||||||||||||||||||||||||||||

VITAL STATISTICS

● **HOW IT GROWS** This plant is naturally globular, however it can grow into a thick column if denied full sunlight.

SHAPE SHIFTER
Rotate the pot every few weeks to prevent golden barrel from leaning towards the light. This can distort its shape.

● **ANATOMY** The main attraction of this cactus is the dense cover of golden yellow spines over the body of the plant. These strong, sharp spines grow at the edges of deep ribs. This plant is solitary, only growing a single, globular body.

● **SIZE** Golden barrel grows quickly at first to reach about 10cm (4in), then grows more slowly. It can eventually reach a diameter of about 60–70cm (24–28in).

Indoors: 60–70cm (24–28in) across

WATER ME
Water me every two weeks or so in spring and summer, when my soil is nearly dry. Don't water me from mid-autumn to early spring.

POSITION ME
I thrive on sunshine so a sunny windowsill or greenhouse is ideal. Keep me above 5°C (41°F) as low temperatures can cause scarring.

SHARE ME

It's best to keep me to yourself as I can only be propagated from seed by cross-pollination. This would be hard to achieve in cultivation with golden barrel.

HELP ME FLOWER

If you keep me healthy I will grow steadily and produce my yellow flowers. I grow these in summer from my crown, once I reach at least the size of a football.

FEED ME

Add a high-potash fertilizer to my water two or three times in the growing period (spring and summer).

REPOT ME

Repot me in early spring into a slightly bigger pot. Use dry compost and don't water me for two weeks afterwards. Wear thick gloves to protect yourself, and wrap a cloth around me to prevent damage to my spines.

I come from Mexico.

ECHINOCEREUS

Echinocereus subinermis

This species, like most of those in the Echinocereus genus, has large, long-lasting flowers. It makes a great showpiece for a wide windowsill in a living room.

VITAL STATISTICS

● **HOW IT GROWS** Globular in shape when young, it slowly becomes columnar and produces a cluster of stems.

ON THE TURN
If grown on a windowsill, give this plant a quarter turn every few weeks, otherwise it will grow lopsided and may topple over.

● **ANATOMY** This cactus has ribbed, dark green or bluish-green stems bearing short, yellow spines, but is in fact the least spiny species in the genus. For this reason, it is sometimes called "unarmed" *Echinocereus*.

● **SIZE** Within a few years this species reaches a height of about 20cm (8in). Each stem will eventually produce a flower, and the blooms are up to 8cm (3in) in diameter.

Indoors: 20cm (8in)

WATER ME
Water me every two weeks or so in spring and summer, when my compost is nearly dry. Don't water me from mid-autumn to spring.

POSITION ME
I will thrive in a sunny position, such as on a south-facing windowsill or in a greenhouse kept frost-free.

HELP ME FLOWER

Expose me to full sunlight in spring and summer and I will produce large, funnel-shaped blooms from an early age. They will last for one or two months in early summer.

SHARE ME

Propagate me by taking cuttings of my young stems. Let them dry for a week, then place them on fresh, dry compost.

REPOT ME

Repot me in early spring every two or three years. Use dry compost and a slightly bigger pot, and don't water me for at least two weeks.

I come from Mexico.

FEED ME

Add a high-potash fertilizer to my water two or three times in spring and summer.

ECHINOCEREUS KNIPPELIANUS

This tiny species forms a low clump up to 8cm (3in) across, composed of dark green spherical stems. It produces pink, purple, or white funnel-shaped flowers.

ECHINOCEREUS VIERECKII MORRICALII

This cactus has almost spineless bright green stems and produces purple funnel-shaped flowers up to 10cm (4in) in diameter.

PEANUT CACTUS

Echinopsis chamaecereus (Chamaecereus sylvestrii)

The peanut cactus has long been a popular choice. It grows rapidly to form clusters of small stems and readily produces attractive, bright red flowers.

VITAL STATISTICS

● **HOW IT GROWS** This is a heavily clustering plant that needs regular repotting to give it room to expand.

PESKY PESTS!

Peanut cactus is very susceptible to red spider mite attack, causing brown discoloration to the stems. Treat as needed (see pp.28–29).

● **ANATOMY** The finger-sized, slightly bristly stems have numerous red flowers in late spring and early summer. It has been extensively hybridized with other *Echinopsis* (formerly *Lobivia*) species to produce slightly thicker stems and differently coloured flowers.

● **SIZE** This cactus grows quickly to produce clusters of narrow stems. Each stem is about 10–15cm (4–6in) long and initially grows upwards before curving downwards. Peanut cactus will rapidly take up the available space in a pot.

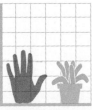

Indoors: 10–15cm (4–6in)

WATER ME

Water me every two weeks or so in spring and summer, when my soil is nearly dry. Don't water me from mid-autumn to spring.

I come from Argentina.

HELP ME FLOWER

When my stems are no more than 8cm (3in) long, they will flower readily if I'm kept in a sunny position.

SHARE ME

Cut off some of my stems in early spring, and place them on fresh, dry compost with a layer of sand. When roots appear, gently insert the cuttings into the compost and water them.

FEED ME

Add a high-potash fertilizer to my water two or three times during the growing period (spring and summer).

POSITION ME

Put me in a sunny position on a windowsill, or in a greenhouse with a minimum temperature of 4°C (39°F).

REPOT ME

Move me in early spring, just before watering commences. Put me into a slightly larger, shallow pot. Use dry compost, and don't water me for about two weeks afterwards.

Echinopsis

Plants in the diverse Echinopsis genus are often hybridized (cross-bred) to produce cacti with a wide range of attractive, colourful flowers.

Large, scented flowers

ECHINOPSIS 'SPRING BLUSH'
This hybrid produces pale pink, scented flowers that can grow up to 16cm (6in) in diameter.

Nocturnal flowers

ECHINOPSIS SUBDENUDATA 'TUFTY'
This hybrid (a spineless form of E. ancistrophora*) has white tufts of wool. It produces big, long-stemmed flowers at night.*

Summer blooms

ECHINOPSIS 'SATURN'
This hybrid produces unusual, peach-coloured flowers. It flowers during the day in summer.

Distinctive stripes

ECHINOPSIS 'GALAXY'
This popular hybrid produces white flowers with a prominent pink stripe on each petal. Blooms can reach 13cm (5in) in diameter.

Deep orange flowers

ECHINOPSIS 'TANGOED'
This hybrid produces striking deep orange flowers with pink-tipped petals. It flowers during the day in summer.

FISHBONE CACTUS

Epiphyllum anguliger

From a genus made up of 12 white-flowered species, the fishbone cactus is often grown in a hanging pot or lined basket to allow its stems to trail.

VITAL STATISTICS

- **HOW IT GROWS** The long, leaf-like stems are not particularly thick, and sprawl downwards as they grow.

PEST CONTROL

These plants can be subject to attack from scale insects, which look like round, brown patches with a slightly raised centre (see pp.28–29).

- **ANATOMY** With its flat, deeply lobed stems, the fishbone cactus can become top-heavy as it grows and needs a substantial pot or a hanging basket. It has strong-smelling, nocturnal, white or pale yellow flowers that are hard to produce indoors.

- **SIZE** The hanging stems continue to lengthen to 1m (3ft) or more if the plant is regularly potted on. By the time they get this long younger shoots will be appearing, and the older stems may be cut off, perhaps for cuttings.

Indoors: 1m (3ft)

WATER ME

Water me every two or three weeks in spring and summer, with an occasional very light watering in autumn and late winter.

POSITION ME

I will scorch in strong, direct sunlight, so I'll need some shade. Indoors, an east- or west-facing windowsill is ideal.

FEED ME

Add a high-potash feed to my water once a month in spring and summer.

HELP ME FLOWER

In the wild I grow in trees, so need dappled sunshine to flower – although too little light will encourage leaf growth instead. I can be reluctant to flower.

SHARE ME

Remove one of my stems and cut it into pieces about 10cm (4in) long. Lay them on fresh, dry compost with a thin layer of sand. Water them once roots appear.

REPOT ME

I need good drainage, so give me a mix of two parts peat or coir to one part bark chippings. Repot me into a slightly larger hanging pot or lined basket in early spring, watering after a week or two.

I come from Mexico.

ERIOSYCE SENILIS

Eriosyce (formerly *Neoporteria*) senilis

An unusual cactus, with its intricate spines and vivid flowers, this species will grow and bloom well in a sunny spot.

||||||||||||||||||||||||||||||||||||||||||||||||||||||||||||||||||||||||||

VITAL STATISTICS

- **HOW IT GROWS** This cactus is globular at first, slowly forming a short, solitary column.

WATER WAYS

Eriosyce is prone to rot if overwatered. If you suspect rot (see p.29), don't water again until the compost has completely dried out.

- **ANATOMY** *Eriosyce senilis* has a ribbed, green-blue body, densely covered with bristly, twisted spines that are usually white. Flowers appear in summer from an early age, often several opening in succession, and each lasting for a week or two.

- **SIZE** *Eriosyce senilis* varies in size from plant to plant but is slow-growing. It can reach 6–18cm (2½–7in) in height and 5–8cm (2–3in) in diameter, taking five years or more to reach this maximum size.

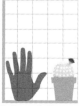

Indoors: 6–18cm (2½–7in)

WATER ME

Water me every three or four weeks (when my compost is nearly dry) in spring and summer, tipping away any excess in the base. Don't water me from mid-autumn to early spring.

POSITION ME

Choose a sunny windowsill or grow in a greenhouse or frame in temperatures no lower than 3–5°C (37–41°F).

SHARE ME

I grow well from seed. If I am placed near other species of *Eriosyce*, the seed I produce may develop into a hybrid of the two species.

HELP ME FLOWER

Given the right care and enough sunlight, I readily produce bold, pink flowers that last for a week or two in spring and summer.

REPOT ME

Transfer me to a new pot in early spring, before watering restarts. Use dry compost and a slightly larger pot.

FEED ME

Give me a high-potash fertilizer two or three times in spring and summer.

I come from Chile.

PERUVIAN OLD LADY

Espostoa melanostele

This striking cactus makes an interesting feature for a large windowsill. Its common name refers to the long, white hairs that cover its stem.

VITAL STATISTICS

● **HOW IT GROWS** This slow-growing cactus gradually forms a clump of columnar stems.

UNDER WRAPS

This spiny plant grows quite big, so when moving or repotting it ask someone to help you. Wrap soft material around the stem to prevent injury.

● **ANATOMY** The ribbed, greyish-green stem produces rows of sharp spines that are yellow in young plants and turn black as the cactus matures. The stem is almost completely hidden by a dense covering of long, white hairs.

● **SIZE** In its natural habitat, this cactus eventually reaches a height of around 2m (6ft), with a width of 10cm (4in). When grown in a container it will reach a height of 25cm (10in) or more within ten years.

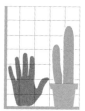

Indoors: 25cm (10in)

WATER ME

Water me every two weeks or so in spring and summer, when my soil is nearly dry. Don't water me from mid-autumn to spring.

POSITION ME

Put me on a sunny windowsill and turn me every few weeks so that I don't grow lopsided and topple over.

HELP ME FLOWER
You'll need to be very patient because I won't bloom until I'm at least 30cm (12in) tall. My white or dull red flowers emerge on the side of my stem, on a thicker patch of wool called the cephalium.

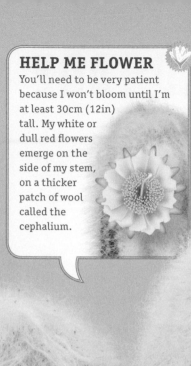

SHARE ME
Propagate me by cutting off some of the shoots that develop around my base. Dry each cutting for a week, then insert into dry compost with the base just below the surface. Support with a stick.

REPOT ME
Do this every two or three years, in early spring. Repot me in dry compost in a slightly bigger pot, and don't water me for at least two weeks afterwards.

I come from Peru.

FEED ME
Add a high-potash fertilizer to my water two or three times during the growing period (spring and summer).

SUZANNE'S SPURGE

Euphorbia suzannae

This plant comes from a genus of over 500 very diverse succulents – from small, round plants to large, tree-like species. They occur in warm climates worldwide.

VITAL STATISTICS

- **HOW IT GROWS** *Euphorbia suzannae* makes a low-growing cluster of stems that spread outwards over time.

- **ANATOMY** This quirky species has separate male and female plants. One of each is needed to achieve pollination and for tiny flowers and seeds to appear on the female plant. This hardy little succulent rarely attracts pests or suffers from disease.

WATCH OUT!

Take care when handling this plant as it contains a toxic, milky-looking sap. Even slight damage will cause the sap to ooze out.

- **SIZE** This plant spreads outwards faster than it grows upwards. It can reach a maximum height of 15cm (6in), but can reach 30cm (12in) across. It is therefore best suited to wide, shallow pots or pans.

Indoors: 15cm (6in)

WATER ME

Water me every two weeks or so in the spring and summer, when my soil is nearly dry. Do not water me from mid-autumn to spring.

POSITION ME

I need sunshine to grow properly, so a sunny windowsill or greenhouse with a minimum temperature of 4°C (39°F) is ideal.

REPOT ME

Repot me in early spring into a slightly bigger shallow pan or pot. Use dry compost and then do not water me for about two weeks.

SHARE ME

Cuttings expose my toxic sap so aren't recommended, but you can grow new plants from my seeds. These are only produced on pollinated female plants. Cover me in fine netting when I'm in fruit, as the capsules that contain my seeds can fire them some distance when ripe!

Female plant has tiny flowers

I come from South Africa.

FEED ME

Add a high-potash fertilizer to my water two or three times in the spring and summer.

MEET THE RELATIVES

PINE CONE PLANT
Euphorbia bupleurifolia
This plant has a roughened, bark-like appearance, with leaves sprouting from the top. It slowly produces offsets and will only leak sap if the leaves are damaged.

BASEBALL PLANT
Euphorbia obesa
This slow-growing species makes a solitary, ball-shaped plant, becoming columnar in time. It is less prone to sap leakage than other species.

WARTY TIGER JAWS

Faucaria tuberculosa

There are several Faucaria species, all but one with bright yellow flowers. This species is named after the "warty" tubercles on its toothed, jaw-like leaves.

VITAL STATISTICS

● **HOW IT GROWS** This plant grows quite quickly to make a cluster of rosettes. It flowers every year.

HOT SPOT!
Too much direct sunlight, especially at the start of the growing season, can scorch the plant. Move it out of direct sun if needed.

● **ANATOMY** Warty tiger jaws has pairs of triangular leaves with soft, tooth-like edges. The leaves form rosettes that produce offsets (young plants). Each rosette produces one spectacular yellow flower in autumn, and the plant may bloom for several months.

● **SIZE** Each rosette grows to about 5cm (2in) across, with clusters of rosettes reaching a spread of about 15cm (6in) after about five years, to cover the surface of a pot 13cm (5in) in diameter.

Indoors: 15cm (6in) across

WATER ME
Water me every two weeks or so in spring and summer, and keep me dry from mid-autumn to early spring.

FEED ME
Feed me once with a high-potash fertilizer in spring.

POSITION ME
I need sun to grow well. A sunny windowsill or a lightly shaded greenhouse or frame is ideal.

HELP ME FLOWER
Given enough sunshine, I produce large, sumptuous flowers in the centre of my "jaws".

SHARE ME
Remove offsets with a sharp knife when repotting me. Place them on compost with a thin layer of sand, inserting them into the surface and watering after about a week.

I come from South Africa.

REPOT ME
It's time to re-home me when I reach the sides of my pot. Do this in early spring, and don't water me for a week or two afterwards.

BABY'S TOES

Fenestraria rhopalophylla subsp. aurantiaca

This unusual-looking plant has brightly coloured flowers. Within a few years it will be large enough to fill a wide, shallow container.

VITAL STATISTICS

- **HOW IT GROWS** This is a stemless plant that gradually produces new leaves to form a low clump.

GENTLY DOES IT
When repotting this plant, wrap a soft cloth around the main clump of leaves and offsets to hold them together and prevent damage.

- **ANATOMY** Each of the small, fleshy, club-shaped leaves of this species has a flattened end in which there is a transparent window-like area that allows light to enter. The toe-like shape of the leaves gave rise to the common name of this plant.

- **SIZE** This dwarf succulent reaches a height of just 5cm (2in), but has a spread of up to 30cm (12in).

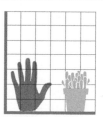

Indoors: 5cm (2in)

WATER ME
Water me every two weeks or so in spring and summer, when my compost is nearly dry. Don't water me from mid-autumn to spring.

POSITION ME
I need a sunny position in order to thrive, such as on a south-facing windowsill or in a frost-free greenhouse.

REPOT ME
When I have spread to fill my pot, repot me in dry compost in a slightly bigger pot. This is best done in early spring. Don't water me for a week or two afterwards.

SHARE ME
Propagate me by gently separating the young offsets that develop around my main cluster of leaves, and placing them on fresh compost. When roots appear, insert them into the compost and start watering a week or two later.

HELP ME FLOWER
If you care for me well, I will produce golden yellow, daisy-like flowers in late summer and autumn.

I come from Namibia.

FEED ME
Add a high-potash fertilizer to my water just once in early spring.

TOP FIVE...

CUTE & COMPACT

If you're looking for a little decoration to add character to a small room or to liven up your workspace, a tiny, slow-growing cactus or succulent might be perfect. They also make great, inexpensive gifts.

1 GYMNOCALYCIUM
Gymnocalycium bruchii
This tiny cactus only grows to about 2–3cm (1–1½in) tall and wide, but clusters quickly. It is easy to care for and flowers at a young age.
See *Gymnocalycium*, pp.88–89.

2 WARTY TIGER JAWS
Faucaria tuberculosa
This striking succulent grows quickly to produce clusters of rosettes. After five years, these can reach a spread of 15cm (6in).
See Warty tiger jaws, pp.76–77.

3 LIVING STONES
Lithops marmorata
'Polepsky smaragd'
The individual stems
of this plant only grow
to about 2.5cm (1in)
tall. It produces white,
daisy-like flowers.
See Living stones, pp.96–97.

4 REBUTIA
Rebutia heliosa
This cactus has small stems about
2cm (¾in) across. It has tiny, silvery
spines and produces bright orange
flowers in spring or early summer.
See *Rebutia heliosa*, p.126.

5 ZEBRA HAWORTHIA
Haworthia attenuata
var. *clariperla*
Popular for its attractive stripes,
this plant grows to about 15cm
(6in) tall. It needs a little shade
to prevent scorched leaves.
See Zebra haworthia, pp.90–91.

DEVIL'S TONGUE

Ferocactus latispinus

This cactus gets its name from its brightly coloured, hooked spines, which resemble pointed tongues. It produces beautiful flowers in summer.

VITAL STATISTICS

● **HOW IT GROWS** Unlike some of its larger relatives, this flat-globular cactus is compact and slow-growing.

● **ANATOMY** The green stem of this solitary-growing species has very prominent ribs. Each of these ribs has clusters of thin, radial spines with about five thicker spines, one of which is sharply hooked.

WATCH OUT!
Wear gloves when repotting this sharp-spined cactus, and for extra protection wrap a thick cloth around the plant.

● **SIZE** After five or six years, this slow-growing cactus is likely to reach about 15cm (6in) in width and about 10cm (4in) in height. At this size, it may start to flower if you're lucky!

Indoors: 10cm (4in)

WATER ME
Water me every two weeks or so in the spring and summer, when my compost is nearly dry. Don't water me from mid-autumn to spring.

POSITION ME
I need to be placed in a sunny spot to grow well and produce flowers. A greenhouse with a minimum temperature of 5°C (41°F) or a south-facing windowsill is ideal.

HELP ME FLOWER

I need full sunlight to produce purple, or sometimes yellow, funnel-shaped blooms from my crown.

REPOT ME

Repot me in early spring into a slightly bigger pot with dry compost. Don't water me for about two weeks afterwards.

SHARE ME

I have just one stem, so if you want more of me you'll need to grow another plant from seed.

FEED ME

Add a high-potash fertilizer to my water two or three times during the growing period (spring and summer).

I come from Mexico.

MEET THE RELATIVES

FEROCACTUS MACRODISCUS

This species has a blue-green stem, yellow or red curved spines, and bright purple-pink flowers. It is of a similar size and shape to devil's tongue, and has the same care needs.

FEROCACTUS HISTRIX

This is a much larger member of the genus. It is one of the most abundant and widespread wild barrel cacti in Mexico, but it can also be grown as a houseplant.

BATES GASTERIA

Gasteria batesiana

This easy-care succulent is an ideal plant for beginners. It has strikingly patterned leaves, attractive flowers, and makes a perfect addition to your windowsill.

VITAL STATISTICS

- **HOW IT GROWS** The leaves of young plants form two opposite rows. With age these grow into a rosette shape.

- **ANATOMY** The dark green, fleshy leaves are triangular or lance-shaped, with raised white spots that give them a rough texture. The leaves take on a reddish hue in bright light.

IT'S TOO BRIGHT!

Unlike many succulents, this plant needs partial shading – the leaves may scorch in full sunlight.

- **SIZE** This succulent is fairly slow-growing, eventually reaching up to 10cm (4in) in height, with a spread of 20cm (8in).

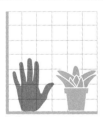

Indoors: 10cm (4in)

WATER ME

Water me every two weeks or so in spring and summer, when my soil is nearly dry. Don't water me at all from mid-autumn to early spring.

POSITION ME

I need bright, indirect light to grow well. A south-east or south-west-facing windowsill, or a partially shaded greenhouse with a minimum temperature of 5°C (41°F) is ideal.

HELP ME FLOWER

I will start to flower each year in late spring or early summer if I am well looked after and once I have formed several leaves. My dangling, reddish-orange blooms are said to resemble tiny stomachs!

Flowers grow on a long, arching stem

SHARE ME

Gently remove any of my young offsets in early summer. Place these on fresh, dry compost, and leave for a week before watering.

LAWYER'S TONGUE
Gasteria bicolor
This species grows up to 50cm (20in) tall, has dark green leaves with white blotches, and produces pink-tipped, green flowers. It requires the same care as its relative.

FEED ME

Include a high-potash fertilizer in my water two or three times in the growing period (spring and summer).

I come from South Africa.

REPOT ME

Repot me after two or three years, when my roots have filled the pot. This is best done in early spring. Use a dry compost and don't water me for two weeks afterwards.

CHIHUAHUA FLOWER

Graptopetalum bellum (formerly *Tacitus bellus*)

This little succulent has graceful, intensely coloured flowers that last for several weeks. It is the perfect decoration for a small windowsill.

VITAL STATISTICS

● **HOW IT GROWS** The leaves of this slow-growing succulent form a flat rosette arrangement.

IT'S TOO HOT!
Don't expose this plant to direct sunlight as its leaves may become scorched.

● **ANATOMY** The rosettes of this plant are made up of thick, fleshy, triangular leaves that are usually slate-grey to dark green in colour and up to 3.5cm (1½in) in length. Within a few years, a number of new rosettes will develop around the original one.

● **SIZE** Each individual rosette is no more than about 8cm (3in) across, but the low cluster of rosettes can be up to 15cm (6in) across.

Indoors: 15cm (6in) across

WATER ME
Water me every two weeks or so in the spring and summer, when my compost is nearly dry. Don't water me in autumn and winter.

POSITION ME
I need bright, indirect light to produce my best leaf colour. An east- or west-facing windowsill, or a greenhouse with a minimum temperature of 5°C (41°F) is ideal.

SHARE ME

Once I have finished flowering, gently remove any of my young offsets. Place these on fresh, dry compost and wait until roots appear before watering.

HELP ME FLOWER

I will produce flowers from late spring to summer if you give me my winter rest. My deep pink, star-shaped blooms are up to 2.5cm (1in) in diameter and grow on short, branching stems.

REPOT ME

Repot me every two or three years, in early spring. Use a slightly bigger pot and dry compost. Don't water me for two weeks afterwards.

FEED ME

Include a high-potash feed in my water two or three times during the growing period (spring and summer).

I come from Mexico.

GYMNOCALYCIUM

Gymnocalycium bruchii

This miniature cactus is easy to care for and great for beginners. Its attractive flowers, which grow readily, make it ideal for a small windowsill.

VITAL STATISTICS

● **HOW IT GROWS** This species quickly produces offsets around the main stem, eventually forming a large, low clump.

CHILD FRIENDLY
The short, bristly spines curve back inward against the stem, so this cactus is unlikely to injure inquisitive children and pets.

● **ANATOMY**
Gymnocalycium species produce some of the finest patterns of spines in the cactus family. This particular species has ribbed, blue-green stems bearing curved, white, bristly spines.

● **SIZE** *Gymnocalycium bruchii* is one of the smallest species in the genus. It grows to 2–3cm (1–1½in) in height and width, and the flowers open up to about the same size in diameter.

Indoors: 2–3cm (1–1½in)

WATER ME
Water me every two weeks or so in spring and summer, when my compost is nearly dry. Don't water me from mid-autumn to spring.

FEED ME
Add a high-potash fertilizer to my water two or three times in spring and summer.

POSITION ME
I will thrive in a sunny spot, such as on a south-facing windowsill or in a greenhouse kept frost-free and above 5°C (41°F).

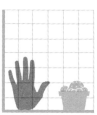

SHARE ME

In early summer, take cuttings of the offsets (young shoots) that develop around my main stems. Leave them to dry for a week and then place them on fresh compost. When roots appear, gently insert them into the compost, and only then start watering.

HELP ME FLOWER

Keep me in bright sunlight and I will produce pale pink flowers in spring and summer from an early age. Every stem will flower within a year or two.

Funnel-shaped flowers

MEET THE RELATIVES

GYMNOCALYCIUM CALOCHLORUM
This plant has wispy spines and pale pink, trumpet-shaped flowers. It reaches a height of 4–6cm (1½–2½in) and needs the same care as G. bruchii.

DWARF CHIN CACTUS
Gymnocalycium baldianum
This species forms an often solitary stem, which grows to 7cm (3in) in height and width. It readily produces its red flowers, and requires the same care as its other relatives.

I come from Argentina.

REPOT ME

This is best done every two or three years in early spring. Repot me in dry compost in a slightly bigger pot. Don't water me for at least two weeks afterwards.

ZEBRA HAWORTHIA

Haworthia attenuata var. *clariperla*

Clariperla is a variation of the Haworthia attenuata species renowned for its distinctive "zebra" stripes. Its appealing markings make it a popular choice.

VITAL STATISTICS

● **HOW IT GROWS** The zebra haworthia produces a cluster of narrow, striped green and cream leaves.

WATER ME
Water me in spring and summer, but only when the soil is nearly dry.

SCORCHING HOT!
This plant will scorch if exposed to too much direct sunlight, but new growth should emerge once it's repositioned.

● **ANATOMY** Each "stripe" is actually made up of a series of small, white tubercles (or nodules). The markings run along the outer surface of each leaf. Other variations of this species have white spotting, rather than regular stripes.

● **SIZE** This plant grows no more than about 15cm (6in) in height or spread. After about five years it will produce enough offsets (young plants) to fill a pot 30cm (12in) in diameter.

Indoors: 15cm (6in)

POSITION ME
I need some sun to grow properly – but not too much. A spot on an east- or west-facing windowsill is perfect.

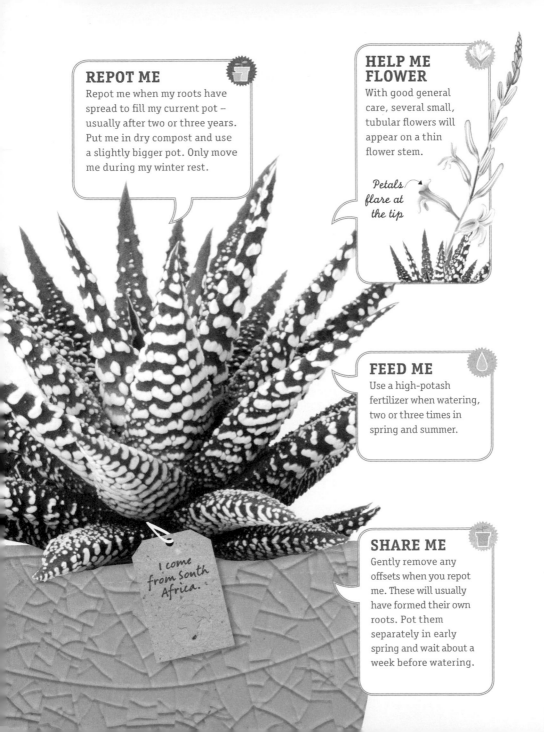

REPOT ME

Repot me when my roots have spread to fill my current pot – usually after two or three years. Put me in dry compost and use a slightly bigger pot. Only move me during my winter rest.

HELP ME FLOWER

With good general care, several small, tubular flowers will appear on a thin flower stem.

Petals flare at the tip

FEED ME

Use a high-potash fertilizer when watering, two or three times in spring and summer.

SHARE ME

Gently remove any offsets when you repot me. These will usually have formed their own roots. Pot them separately in early spring and wait about a week before watering.

I come from South Africa.

PANDA PLANT

Kalanchoe tomentosa

This plant is named after its "furry" brown-tipped leaves. It comes from a genus of about 150 succulents, ranging from small shrubs to big, branching plants.

VITAL STATISTICS

● **HOW IT GROWS** The relatively fast-growing panda plant forms a branching, shrubby structure.

WATER STORAGE
The leaves of the panda plant are covered in short, silvery hairs, which reflect light and minimize water loss.

● **ANATOMY** This plant has thick, fleshy, grey-green leaves with brown edges, each up to 9cm (3½in) long. They have a soft, felt-like covering. Panda plants can flower, although this is quite rare indoors where the plant is usually grown for its attractive foliage.

● **SIZE** After a year or two, this succulent will have become about 30–40cm (12–16in) tall, with side branches. After five or more years, it may reach 60cm (24in) in height.

Indoors: 60cm (24in)

WATER ME
Water me in spring and summer, but not at all from mid-autumn to early spring. Before watering, check that my compost is nearly dry.

FEED ME
Add a high-potash fertilizer to my water two or three times during the growing period (spring and summer).

POSITION ME
I need some sunshine to grow properly. A windowsill or a lightly shaded greenhouse with a minimum temperature of 4°C (39°F) is ideal.

HELP ME FLOWER

I rarely flower indoors, so don't be too disappointed if I don't bloom. Clusters of several tubular red flowers may appear on a stem in spring.

SHARE ME

Share me by removing my offsetting branches in spring or summer. Place them on fresh, dry compost with a layer of sand. Support the tiny plants with a stick, and only water once roots appear.

REPOT ME

Move me into a slightly bigger pot when my roots have filled my current pot (every two or three years). It is best to do this in early spring. Don't water me for at least two weeks afterwards.

I come from Madagascar.

MEET THE RELATIVES

DESERT SURPRISE
Kalanchoe humilis
This species has attractive pale green leaves with bold, maroon-striped markings. Outside it can grow 90cm (36in) tall, but it is usually shorter as a houseplant.

FLAMING KATY
Kalanchoe blossfeldiana
This popular relative of the panda plant is sold in flower all year round. The flowers are red, but hybrids have been bred with pink, orange, white, or yellow flowers.

AGAVE CACTUS

Leuchtenbergia principis

This slow-growing Mexican cactus is the only Leuchtenbergia species. It has long, harmless, papery spines.

VITAL STATISTICS

● **HOW IT GROWS** The agave cactus is a solitary plant. The base becomes increasingly woody with age.

A GOOD DRINK

Water regularly and well to prevent dieback at the tips of the tubercles (but only once the compost is dry from the previous soaking).

● **ANATOMY** This plant has long, thin, green tubercles that resemble a rosette of leaves. The spines are long, papery, and grow at the tips of the tubercles. The growth of this cactus can be stunted by a lack of nutrients or water.

● **SIZE** The agave cactus grows very slowly, taking about four years to reach flowering size. It eventually reaches about 25cm (10in) in height and spread.

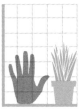

Indoors: 25cm (10in)

WATER ME

Water me every two weeks or so in spring and summer, when my soil is nearly dry. Do not water me from mid-autumn to spring.

POSITION ME

I need sunshine to grow properly, so a south-facing windowsill is the perfect spot.

SHARE ME
You might have to keep me all to yourself! I rarely produce offsets and will need to be pollinated to seed.

HELP ME FLOWER
I need to be kept healthy to produce my bright yellow flowers. These grow from my crown once I've formed at least 15 spined tubercles.

FEED ME
Add a high-potash fertilizer to my water two or three times in the growing period (spring and summer).

REPOT ME
Repot me in early spring into a slightly bigger pot. Use dry compost and then do not water me for about two weeks afterwards.

I come from Mexico.

LIVING STONES

Lithops marmorata 'Polepsky smaragd'

Living stones are fascinating plants that mimic the stones found in their rocky native habitat. 'Polepsky smaragd' is green or yellow-green in colour.

VITAL STATISTICS

- **HOW IT GROWS** This plant makes a cluster of small two-leaved stems that spread quite quickly.

WATER WORRIES

Living stones need careful watering. Too much water may split the stems, which will cause scarring once they heal.

- **ANATOMY** Each stem is divided into two swollen leaves or lobes, and each stem may produce two more stems per year until a many-headed clump forms. The current year's stems shrivel away over winter. White flowers emerge in summer or autumn.

- **SIZE** Each part of this plant grows to no more than about 2.5cm (1in) tall and 3cm (1¼in) wide, but it will slowly cover the surface of a wide, shallow pot as it produces offsets (young plants).

Indoors: 2.5cm (1in)

WATER ME

Wait until my old stem has completely shrivelled before starting to water in spring or early summer. Continue every two or three weeks, but only when my soil is dry. Stop again in early winter.

POSITION ME

I need sunshine to grow properly. A sunny windowsill works well, or a lightly shaded greenhouse kept above 4°C (39°F).

HELP ME FLOWER

With the right care I will flower every year. Buds appear in the centre of each of my stems and open fully from mid-autumn to early winter.

SHARE ME

I grow well from seed (see p.27). If seeds aren't available, a trickier method is to remove my offsets with a sharp knife below the stem when you repot me.

I come from South Africa.

FEED ME

Add a high-potash fertilizer to my water just once at the start of the growing period in late spring.

REPOT ME

Only repot me when I reach the sides of my pot. Do this at the start of the growing season in late spring, then don't water me for a week or two afterwards.

OLD LADY CACTUS

Mammillaria hahniana

One of a huge genus of popular plants, numbering over 170 species, the old lady cactus is named after its white, hair-like spines and bristles.

VITAL STATISTICS

● **HOW IT GROWS** The old lady cactus is globular. It can be solitary or form sizeable clumps.

GOOD CARE
Don't water it too much, and give this cactus full exposure to sunlight. If growing on a windowsill, turn the pot every few weeks so it grows evenly.

● **ANATOMY** This cactus is covered with dense, white bristles and spines. The stem underneath is light green in colour. Pink flowers are readily produced in a ring at the top of the stem in late spring and summer.

● **SIZE** Size varies greatly within the *Mammillaria* genus from tiny acorn-sized stems to large, football-sized ones. Each stem of the old lady cactus can grow about 10cm (4in) tall.

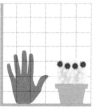
Indoors: 10cm (4in)

WATER ME
Only water me in spring and summer. Do this about every two weeks, but only when the compost is nearly dry.

POSITION ME
I need lots of sunshine to flourish, either on a windowsill or in a greenhouse with a minimum temperature of 5°C (41°F).

HELP ME FLOWER

A ring of pink flowers will form near the top of my stem. As long as I have a winter rest period, not too much water, and plenty of sunshine, I will reliably produce a wonderful show of blooms.

MEET THE RELATIVES ▶

SHARE ME

If I form clusters, take cuttings of my surrounding offsets (young plants). I can also be raised from seed instead.

REPOT ME

Repot me in early spring, using dry compost and a slightly larger pot. Don't water for at least two weeks afterwards.

I come from Mexico.

FEED ME

Add a high-potash fertilizer to my water two or three times in the growing period (spring and summer).

Mammillaria

Mammillaria cacti come from North and South America. Most species flower easily, making them a great choice for beginner cactus growers.

WHAT'S IN A NAME?
Mammillaria are often called "pincushion" cacti because of their round shape and numerous spines.

Pink flowers grow on long stems

MAMMILLARIA LONGIFLORA
This is one of the most popular species, producing large, pink flowers in summer. Watch out for the long, hooked spines.

Flowers can also be cream or red

MEXICAN PINCUSHION
Mammillaria magnimamma
This large species makes a
cluster of stems, each about
10cm (4in) in width. If given
enough space, it can reach
60cm (24in) or more across.

Flowers form ring shape

CARMEN'S PINCUSHION
Mammillaria carmenae
This tiny plant is densely
covered with yellow spines.
The globular stems only reach
5cm (2in) in width and cluster
as the plant grows.

White or pink flowers emerge in winter

FEATHER CACTUS
Mammillaria plumosa
This cactus has soft, feather-like
spines. The close-packed, clumping
stems are each about 6–7cm
(2–2½in) in width.

Small, pale yellow flowers

LACE CACTUS
Mammillaria elongata
This popular species has long stems
and usually has brown spines. It is
very easy to propagate from
stem cuttings.

MATUCANA

Matucana madisoniorum

This plant comes from a genus of about a dozen cacti. They are all native to the Peruvian Andes, some species growing at altitudes of up to 3,000m (10,000ft).

VITAL STATISTICS

- **HOW IT GROWS** This cactus starts off globular, but can become slightly columnar with age.

FRAGILE!
The delicate spines on this plant are lightly attached and prone to dropping off. Take care when handling.

- **ANATOMY** *Matucana madisoniorum* has a very distinctive look, with a smooth, green body and few spines. The spines grow in clumps, and are curved and needle-like. Although this cactus rarely suffers from pests or disease, it is prone to rot if overwatered.

- **SIZE** Size varies from species to species in this genus. As a houseplant, *Matucana madisoniorum* eventually grows to about 30cm (12in) in height and 15cm (6in) in width. It grows fairly quickly and flowers at an early age.

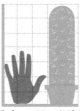

Indoors: 30cm (12in)

WATER ME
Water me every two weeks or so in spring and summer, when my soil is nearly dry. Don't water me from mid-autumn to spring.

POSITION ME
I need sunshine to grow properly, so a sunny windowsill or greenhouse with a minimum temperature of 4°C (39°F) is ideal.

HELP ME FLOWER

I need to be kept healthy to produce my bright red flowers in summer. These grow from my crown when my stem has reached about 8–10cm (3–4in).

SHARE ME

You might have to keep me all to yourself! This species rarely produces offsets (young plants), so new plants must be grown from seed.

FEED ME

Add a high-potash fertilizer to my water two or three times in the growing period (spring and summer).

REPOT ME

Repot me in early spring into a slightly bigger pot, being careful not to knock off my spines. Use dry compost and then wait two weeks before watering.

I come from Peru.

MATUCANA POLZII

This member of the genus puts most of its energy into producing offsets, which makes it very easy to propagate. However, it rarely produces flowers.

MATUCANA KRAHNII

Like its relative, this species also produces bright red flowers from its crown. It may produce several sets of flowers in spring and summer.

DWARF TURK'S CAP

Melocactus matanzanus

The defining characteristic of this popular genus is the "cephalium", a woolly topknot that produces tiny flowers. This species is one of the smaller of the genus.

VITAL STATISTICS

- **HOW IT GROWS** The round body of this plant grows first, followed by the distinctive cephalium.

- **ANATOMY** The cephalium is a colourful structure made of wool and bristles, which produces flowers and fruit. The fruits are tubular and have a waxy texture. In some wild species, the cephalium has been known to grow over 1m (3ft) tall!

KEEP ME WARM!
This plant, along with others in the genus, is used to tropical climates, so always keep it above 10°C (50°F).

- **SIZE** Dwarf Turk's cap grows to about 10cm (4in) in height before forming the cephalium. By comparison, most other species will grow to about 25–40cm (10–15in) across, and a little taller.

Indoors: 10cm (4in)

WATER ME
Only water me in the spring and summer months, when my soil is nearly dry (every two weeks or so).

POSITION ME
I need sunshine to grow properly, so a sunny windowsill is ideal – but don't shut me behind curtains on cold nights!

SHARE ME

Although I rarely have offsets (young plants), I do often produce fruit. You can grow seeds from these fairly easily – although you'll need to be patient as growth is slow!

HELP ME FLOWER
Keep me growing healthily, with correct feeding and watering, to ensure my cephalium forms – tiny pink flowers grow from this woolly structure.

Flowers grow from the woolly cephalium

REPOT ME
Repot me in early spring into a slightly bigger pot. Use dry compost and then don't water me for about two weeks.

I come from Cuba.

FEED ME
Add a high-potash fertilizer to my water two or three times during spring and summer.

ANGEL'S WINGS

Opuntia microdasys alba

Angel's wings is the only cactus in this very large genus with spines that are not barbed. It is a small plant comprising wing-like, jointed pads.

VITAL STATISTICS

● **HOW IT GROWS** Over a few years, angel's wings forms a branching plant of flattened pads as wide as it is tall.

SAFE OPTION

This plant has harmless spines, but beware of lookalike white-spined versions of *O. microdasys*, which do have nasty spines.

● **ANATOMY** Angel's wings has oval, mid-green pads covered with soft, white spines. New pads branch from the top of older ones to produce a bushy plant. Younger pads may dry up in winter. If this happens, remove them then water earlier than usual in spring.

● **SIZE** Over a few years this cactus will slowly branch to reach a modest 20cm (8in) in height and spread. At this point, if grown indoors, it is likely to be top-heavy and will need replacing. Use younger pads to form new plants.

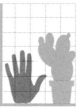

Indoors: 20cm (8in)

WATER ME

Water me every other week in spring and summer when the compost is nearly dry. Don't water me from mid-autumn to spring.

POSITION ME

I thrive in a sunny spot, in temperatures above 5°C (41°F), on a windowsill or in a greenhouse.

HELP ME FLOWER

Put me in a sunny spot and I will flower in summer once I am a few years old. Unlike many other species of *Opuntia*, I flower quite readily.

SHARE ME

Remove some of my pads, cutting at the joint with a sharp knife. Allow the cut surfaces to dry then lay them flat on fresh compost with a light covering of sand, watering when roots start to emerge.

BEAVERTAIL CACTUS
Opuntia basilaris
This species has blue-grey pads and pink flowers. The bristles, or glochids, are very painful to touch and hard to remove from bare skin.

REPOT ME

In early spring, repot me into a slightly bigger pot with dry compost. Wait for at least two weeks before watering.

I come from Mexico.

FEED ME

Add a high-potash fertilizer to my water two or three times in spring and summer.

COW'S TONGUE CACTUS
Opuntia engelmannii
This has green, sometimes blue-green, pads and yellow or reddish flowers. Be warned that it has vicious barbed spines and is best not grown indoors or anywhere near children.

TOP FIVE...
TRAILING PLANTS

These unusual plants make great features in your home. Their long stems come in many shapes and can grow to impressive lengths. They are best displayed in a hanging pot or lined basket.

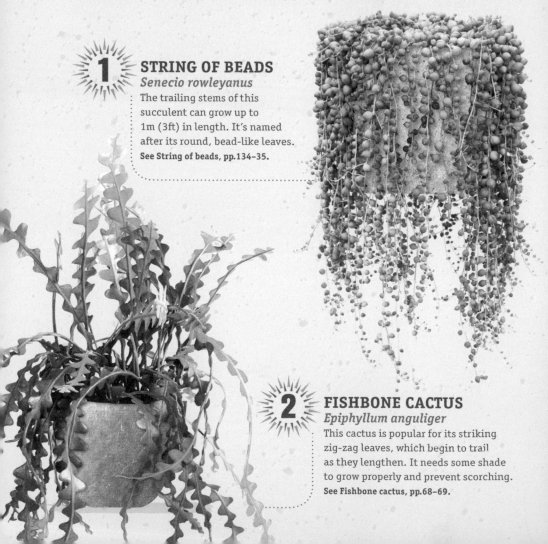

1 STRING OF BEADS
Senecio rowleyanus
The trailing stems of this succulent can grow up to 1m (3ft) in length. It's named after its round, bead-like leaves.
See String of beads, pp.134–35.

2 FISHBONE CACTUS
Epiphyllum anguliger
This cactus is popular for its striking zig-zag leaves, which begin to trail as they lengthen. It needs some shade to grow properly and prevent scorching.
See Fishbone cactus, pp.68–69.

3 RAT'S TAIL CACTUS
Disocactus flagelliformis
This plant must be kept out of too much direct sunlight to thrive. Its long, thin stems can reach 1m (3ft) in length.
See Rat's tail cactus, pp.56–57.

4 DONKEY'S TAIL
Sedum morganianum
'Harry Butterfield'
The stems of this succulent can reach 60cm (24in) in length. Take care when handling, as the leaves can be easily knocked off.
See Donkey's tail, pp.130–31.

5 MONKEY'S TAIL
Cleistocactus winteri colademono
This very popular cactus was only recently discovered. The long, furry stems are covered in soft spines that can be gently stroked – but only downwards.
See Monkey's tail, pp.46–47.

STARFISH FLOWER

Orbea (formerly Stapelia) variegata

Named after its mottled, star-shaped flowers, this cactus-like succulent is a member of the popular Orbea genus, which has more than 60 species.

VITAL STATISTICS

- **HOW IT GROWS** The starfish flower produces a cluster of stems and is a fast and prolific grower.

- **ANATOMY** Like all species in the genus, the starfish flower grows rows of blunt "teeth" in the upper part of each stem. It has particularly attractive flowers, with others in the species varying in colour from red and brown to green and yellow.

WHAT'S THAT SMELL?
The flowers may look great, but their odour is less appealing! As this plant is pollinated by flies, the flowers emit a bad smell to attract them.

- **SIZE** Rarely growing to more than about 15cm (6in) in both height and spread, a "parent" starfish flower will eventually produce enough offsets (young plants) to fill a pot 30cm (12in) in diameter.

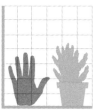

Indoors: 15cm (6in)

WATER ME
Water me about every two weeks in spring and summer – but only when my soil is nearly dry. Don't water me from mid-autumn onwards.

POSITION ME
I need some sunshine to grow properly, but not too much – a south-east- or south-west-facing windowsill is ideal.

HELP ME FLOWER

My distinctive flowers appear at the base of the stem on new, outer shoots. They will grow readily once a few stems have developed.

SHARE ME

Share me by gently removing any offsets when you repot me. Also, if the centre of a clump has died out, break the undamaged parts into smaller clumps and pot on.

FEED ME

Add a high-potash fertilizer to my water two or three times during the growing period.

REPOT ME

Repot me when my stems have covered the surface of the pot – but only during winter. Use dry compost and don't water me for at least two weeks and until early spring.

I come from South Africa.

OREOCEREUS

Oreocereus leucotrichus

Sometimes known as old man of the Andes, this cactus is one of a small genus of six species. It is densely covered with spines and hairs.

VITAL STATISTICS

● **HOW IT GROWS** This is usually a clustering cactus that forms a sturdy clump of columns over time.

STRONG SPINES

This plant's spines are attractive but sharp. When handling, wrap the stem in soft material to avoid hurting the spines – or your hands!

● **ANATOMY** Each stem has 10–15 ribs. Offsets grow at the base when the plant is 10cm (4in) tall. Showy, red flowers emerge through a thick patch of wool-like hairs on the side of the column near the growing point. Rotate this cactus to keep growth straight.

● **SIZE** *Oreocereus leucotrichus* grows to about 60cm (2ft) after ten years of good care. It can eventually reach 1m (3ft) in height, with a stem diameter of about 10cm (4in).

Indoors: 1m (3ft)

WATER ME

Water me in spring and summer, every two weeks or so when the soil is nearly dry. Don't give me any water from mid-autumn to spring.

FEED ME

Include a high-potash fertilizer in my water two or three times in the growing period.

POSITION ME

Full sunlight on a windowsill or in a greenhouse will allow me to grow well and produce a good covering of spines.

HELP ME FLOWER

Full sunlight helps me produce my deep red, funnel-shaped flowers. These grow in summer from the top of my stem, once I have reached a height of 60cm (2ft).

SHARE ME

Once offsets are about 15cm (6in) tall they may be removed in early summer with a sharp knife and left to dry. Prop them up on fresh, dry compost with a layer of sand and only start watering when roots appear at the base.

REPOT ME

Repot me in early spring into a slightly bigger pot. Use dry compost and wait at least two weeks before watering me.

I come from Peru and Chile.

MOONSTONES

Pachyphytum oviferum

The unusual egg-shaped leaves give this succulent its species name oviferum. It is also known as sugared almond plant due to the blue-white bloom on its leaves.

VITAL STATISTICS

● **HOW IT GROWS** This plant branches and makes a clump of stems, each with its own cluster of leaves.

LEAVING A MARK

Pachyphytums have a coating of farina (a fine powder-like substance), which will mark or rub off if handled.

● **ANATOMY** This succulent forms rosettes of its fleshy leaves. Each leaf is 3–5cm (1¼–2in) long and 3cm (1¼in) wide. The leaves often grow tightly packed. Gaps can appear between the leaves if the plant isn't getting enough light.

● **SIZE** With the right care, clumps of moonstones may grow to 20cm (8in) long and sprawl to about 30cm (12in) in diameter over the course of eight to ten years.

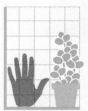

Indoors: 20cm (8in)

WATER ME

Water me every two weeks in spring and summer, but only when my soil is nearly dry. Don't water me from mid-autumn onwards.

POSITION ME

I need sunshine to grow properly. A sunny windowsill or a greenhouse with a minimum temperature of 4°C (39°F) is ideal.

SHARE ME

To share me, remove some of my leaves, keeping the base of each one intact. Lay them on dry, fresh compost with a thin layer of sand. They will send out roots and a tiny rosette will form.

HELP ME FLOWER

Keep me healthy to encourage my flowers. These grow on a long, elegant stem, which can reach a height of 30cm (12in).

PACHYPHYTUM COMPACTUM

This species has more cylindrical leaves than moonstones, often with purple tips. The flowers are yellow to pinkish-orange. It grows in rosettes.

REPOT ME

Move me into a slightly larger pot of dry compost every two or three years, during the spring. Don't water me for two weeks afterwards.

I come from Mexico.

FEED ME

Include a high-potash fertilizer in my water two or three times in spring and summer.

PACHYPHYTUM HOOKERI

Another compact, rosette-forming species, this has longer, tapering leaves and coral-coloured flowers.

GOLDEN POWDER PUFF

Parodia chrysacanthion

This cactus is easy to grow, and its striking appearance and brightly coloured flowers make it a perfect windowsill decoration.

VITAL STATISTICS

● **HOW IT GROWS** An initially globular cactus, this will cluster slowly after a few years.

EXTRA CARE
The fine, delicate spines of this plant are easily damaged – even with a cloth placed around it – so take extra care when repotting.

● **ANATOMY** The stem of this species has spirally arranged ribs and a dense covering of fine, golden spines. The crown of the plant is covered with very slim, pale yellow spines – hence the common name of this cactus.

● **SIZE** This slow-growing plant grows up to 13cm (5in) in height and 10cm (4in) in width. Offsets (young stems) develop around the main stem, eventually forming an impressive cluster.

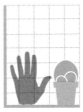

Indoors: 13cm (5in)

WATER ME
Water me every two weeks or so in spring and summer, when my compost is nearly dry. Water me occasionally from mid-autumn to spring, too.

POSITION ME
I need bright light to grow properly. A windowsill or lightly shaded greenhouse kept above 5°C (41°F) is ideal.

HELP ME FLOWER

A cooling period during winter helps me to flower the following spring. From an early age I produce golden yellow, funnel-shaped blooms at my crown.

SHARE ME

This species is usually grown from seed, but you can take cuttings from the offsets that develop around my stem. Dry them for a week, then place them on fresh compost. When roots appear, insert them into the compost, and start watering.

PARODIA SUBTERRANEA

The flowers of this species are deep red, and white wool grows around the crown of the plant. This cactus requires the same care as its relative.

I come from Argentina.

REPOT ME

Repot me every two or three years, in early spring. Use dry compost in a slightly bigger pot, and don't water me for at least two weeks afterwards.

FEED ME

Add a high-potash fertilizer to my water two or three times during spring and summer.

YELLOW TOWER

Parodia (formerly Notocactus) leninghausii

When mature, yellow tower forms a handsome, clustering showpiece. It is part of the Notocactus group, which has recently been added to the Parodia genus.

VITAL STATISTICS

● **HOW IT GROWS** This starts as a young globular plant, becoming columnar then clustering freely from the base.

TAKE TURNS
Rotate plants on a windowsill a quarter of a turn the same way every few weeks, or they may lean towards the light and even topple over.

● **ANATOMY** The globular then columnar body has about 30 ribs covered with soft, golden spines. Large, bright yellow flowers are produced at the apex once the plant is about 10cm (4in) tall – or before if you're lucky.

● **SIZE** The columnar stem of yellow tower grows to 30cm (12in) tall or more, and the mature plant starts to cluster from the base to make an impressive group. Regular repotting will keep it growing steadily.

Indoors: 30cm (12in)

WATER ME

Water me every two weeks or when the compost is nearly dry in spring and summer only. If my roots look brown when you repot me, cut them back to the white tissue (this is a sign that I'm having too much water).

POSITION ME

I need a sunny position to flourish, such as on a south-facing windowsill or in a greenhouse or frame above 5°C (41°F).

SHARE ME

Cut away one of my clustering stems in summer, when it's two or three years old. Dry it for a week then put it on fresh compost with a thin layer of sand. When roots appear, insert it into the soil and start watering.

HELP ME FLOWER

Expose me to plenty of sunlight and I'll flower in spring and summer. I produce several flowers over a period of a week or two.

REPOT ME

Move me into a slightly larger pot in early spring. Repot me into dry compost, and only water me again after about two weeks.

FEED ME

Give me a high-potash fertilizer two or three times in spring and summer.

I come from Brazil.

MEET THE RELATIVES

BALL CACTUS
Parodia magnifica
This species clusters after about ten years to form a clump of fat, globular stems that will eventually fill a pot 30cm (12in) in diameter. Its spines are soft, thin, and bristly.

SILVER BALL
Parodia scopa
With much smaller stems than its relative, this cactus will make a large cluster, growing to about 50cm (20in) across after ten years. It is covered with white or pale brown spines.

BLUE TORCH

Pilosocereus pachycladus

Blue torch is a very striking blue columnar cactus from Brazil. Its relatives are found in the wild from northern South America to the southern United States.

VITAL STATISTICS

- **HOW IT GROWS** This slow-growing columnar cactus is solitary to 90cm (36in) before clustering from the base.

IN THE WILD
Beautiful in a pot, this cactus is truly spectacular in the wild, with a potential height as a branching, tree-like plant of 10m (33ft)!

- **ANATOMY** The attractive appearance of this cactus comes from its elegant shape, and its blue-silver, almost turquoise stems with contrasting yellow spines. It has 5–19 ribs. Overwatering can cause root-rot and the loss of the plant.

- **SIZE** Within eight years, blue torch should grow to about 60cm (24in) in height. Regularly repot to ensure constant growth and rotate the pot a little every few weeks to keep the columns growing vertically.

Indoors: 60cm (24in)

WATER ME

Water me every two weeks or so in spring and summer, when my soil is nearly dry. Don't water me from mid-autumn to spring.

REPOT ME
Repot me in early spring into a slightly bigger pot. Use fresh, dry compost and don't water me for at least two weeks. Wear thick gloves to protect yourself, and wrap a cloth around me to prevent damage to my spines.

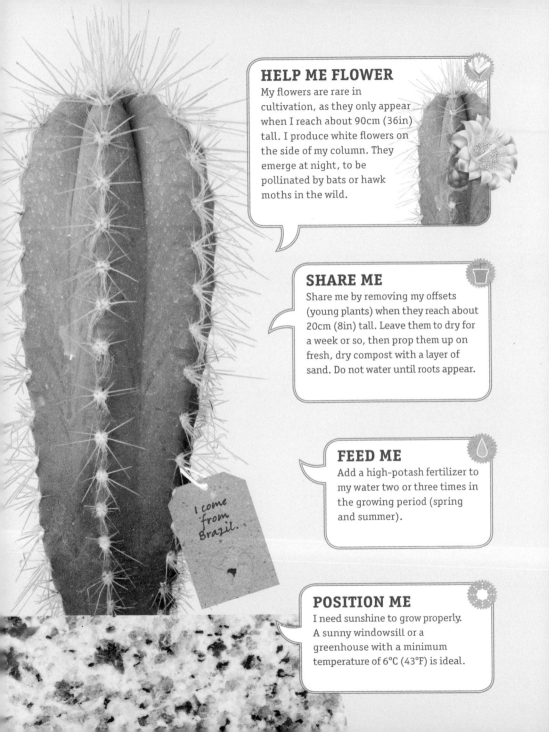

HELP ME FLOWER

My flowers are rare in cultivation, as they only appear when I reach about 90cm (36in) tall. I produce white flowers on the side of my column. They emerge at night, to be pollinated by bats or hawk moths in the wild.

SHARE ME

Share me by removing my offsets (young plants) when they reach about 20cm (8in) tall. Leave them to dry for a week or so, then prop them up on fresh, dry compost with a layer of sand. Do not water until roots appear.

FEED ME

Add a high-potash fertilizer to my water two or three times in the growing period (spring and summer).

POSITION ME

I need sunshine to grow properly. A sunny windowsill or a greenhouse with a minimum temperature of 6°C (43°F) is ideal.

I come from Brazil.

PYGMAEOCEREUS

Pygmaeocereus bylesianus

A tiny, short columnar cactus, this is one of only two Pygmaeocereus species. It has large, white, nocturnal flowers that bloom for a single night.

VITAL STATISTICS

● **HOW IT GROWS** This short columnar cactus steadily produces offsets (young plants) to form a cluster of stems.

MOTH MAGNET
The flowers are borne above the cactus on long stems and have a strange, not unpleasant scent to attract pollinators such as moths.

● **ANATOMY** Each dark green, columnar stem has 12–17 ribs and short, pale to dark brown spines. The many offsets branch from the base. White flowers appear on the stems, blooming at dusk or in the dark.

● **SIZE** The individual columns grow up to 8cm (3in) tall and each may be 2cm (¾in) in diameter. The flower stems are usually about 6cm (2½in) long.

Indoors: 8cm (3in)

WATER ME
Water me only in spring and summer every two weeks or so, and not until the compost is nearly dry. Don't water me from mid-autumn to early spring.

POSITION ME
I thrive in a sunny location on a windowsill or greenhouse, with a temperature no lower than 5°C (41°F).

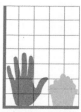

SHARE ME

Make new plants by removing a few of my offsets in early summer when they are at least 5cm (2in) long. Place them on compost with a thin layer of sand. Start watering when roots appear, and then insert the cuttings gently into the compost.

HELP ME FLOWER

Place me in a sunny spot and I can produce beautiful, large, white flowers typical of those seen on many taller-growing relatives with "cereus" as part of their name.

FEED ME

Give me a high-potash fertilizer two or three times with water in spring and summer.

I come from Peru.

REPOT ME

Move me to a slightly bigger pot in winter, before watering starts again in spring. Don't water me for at least two weeks afterwards.

CROWN CACTUS

Rebutia krainziana

This cactus produces brightly coloured flowers. Cacti from this genus flower easily in spring and summer, making them popular houseplants.

||||||||||||||||||||||||||||||||||||||||||||||||||||||||||||||||||||||

VITAL STATISTICS

● **HOW IT GROWS** *Rebutia krainziana* is globular and grows quite quickly to make a cluster of stems.

KEEP REPOTTING

Repotting every year at first, then every two or three years once mature, will encourage more stems and more flowers.

● **ANATOMY** The stems of this cactus are dark green with contrasting white spines. In spring, once mature, each stem produces a number of flowers from the base. The flowers are usually red but may be yellow, orange, or white.

● **SIZE** This species starts as a young globular plant and grows into clusters after a few years. It spreads outwards, but never reaches more than about 5cm (2in) tall.

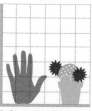

Indoors: 5cm (2in)

WATER ME

Water me every two weeks or so in spring and summer when my compost is nearly dry. Ease off in early autumn, and do not water at all in late autumn and winter.

POSITION ME

I need sunshine to grow properly, so a sunny windowsill or greenhouse with a minimum temperature of 4°C (39°F) is ideal.

HELP ME FLOWER

Keep me healthy and I'll produce bright red flowers in spring. These appear from the base of my stems when I am about 3cm (1¼in) tall.

SHARE ME

Gently remove my offsets (young plants) when they are at least 2cm (¾in) tall. Leave these to dry for about a week before placing on fresh compost and a layer of sand. Water once roots form.

I come from Argentina and Bolivia.

REPOT ME

In early spring, repot me in a slightly bigger pot with dry compost. Wait for at least two weeks before watering.

FEED ME

Add a high-potash fertilizer to my water two or three times during the growing period (spring and summer).

MEET THE RELATIVES

Rebutia

Cacti from this genus are particularly popular as they easily produce flowers in a range of colours. They also offset regularly, making them easy to propagate.

Bright orange flowers with a yellow centre

MOUNTAIN AIR

Rebutia are mountain plants that need good ventilation to prevent them from scorching in the sun.

REBUTIA HELIOSA

This unusual species has small stems about 2cm (¾in) across. These are densely covered with tiny, silvery spines. Flowers cover the plant in spring.

Yellow flowers

REBUTIA SENILIS
This popular cactus is named after its dense, white spines. It is capable of self-fertilization, and its seed pods form at the base of the stem. Flowers can be yellow, red, orange, or white.

White daisy-like flowers

REBUTIA ALBIFLORA
The stems of this species only grow to about 2.5cm (1in) in width, but rapidly form a tight cluster. Its pretty, white flowers are produced readily in summer.

Bright orange flowers

REBUTIA FLAVISTYLA
This cactus has quite large stems, about 5cm (2in) in width. It is easy to propagate from offsets.

Violet flowers

REBUTIA VIOLACIFLORA
This species gets its name from the violet colour of its flowers. It is similar in size to Rebutia flavistyla.

CHRISTMAS CACTUS

Schlumbergera (formerly Zygocactus) truncata

An easy-to-grow favourite that thrives on a windowsill, this cactus flowers late in the year, at around Christmas time.

VITAL STATISTICS

- **HOW IT GROWS** This is a trailing plant with flattened stems that droop over the sides of the pot.

SHADY SPOT
In the wild this dwells on trees or in shady, rocky places, so take care not to expose the stems to too much direct sunshine.

- **ANATOMY** Fresh, scallop-edged segments appear at the end of each branch to form a chain that lengthens and trails downwards. The buds appear at the tips of the newest segments, then elongate before bursting into flower.

- **SIZE** Over a few years, several stems will form from the base, each lengthening to 30cm (12in) or more. It may grow slowly if it doesn't have enough water or food, or if it's in too much shade, but with the right care it can live for several decades.

Indoors: 30cm (12in)

WATER ME
Water me in the spring and summer, easing off in early autumn. Don't water me after I flower in the winter months.

POSITION ME
I need dappled sun to grow properly, so a south-east- or south-west-facing windowsill is ideal.

HELP ME FLOWER

Follow my care advice and pink buds, followed by flowers, will appear in autumn or early winter on stems that have grown new segments.

SHARE ME

Make cuttings at my stem joints and let them dry for a few days. Place them on compost, inserting each cutting gently into the soil when roots appear.

MEET THE RELATIVE

EASTER CACTUS
Hatiora gaertneri
This forms a larger plant than its relative, with segments that are less sharply toothed. It flowers in late spring.

FEED ME

Give me a high-potash fertilizer with my water two or three times in the growing period.

I come from Brazil.

REPOT ME

When my roots have filled the pot, repot me after I've flowered. Use a dry mix of two parts acid compost (peat or coir) and one part bark chippings, and don't water me until early spring.

DONKEY'S TAIL

Sedum morganianum 'Harry Butterfield'

This very popular trailing succulent and its several hybrids – one of which is illustrated here – needs a hanging pot to truly show it off.

VITAL STATISTICS

- **HOW IT GROWS** Donkey's tail produces a succession of leaf-covered stems, which start to hang as they grow.

- **ANATOMY** This fleshy, evergreen succulent produces blue-green leaves tightly packed along trailing stems. Each year, small clusters of flowers emerge from the new growth at the end of the mature stems.

HANDLE WITH CARE

Too much handling can result in leaves being damaged or knocked off, as they are lightly attached.

- **SIZE** The hanging stems of this plant lengthen to 60cm (24in) or more if regularly potted on. By the time they are this long younger shoots will be appearing, and the older stems may be removed and used for cuttings.

Indoors: 60cm (24in)

WATER ME

Water me every two weeks or so in spring and summer, when my soil is dry. Don't water me from early autumn to early spring – to give me a winter rest.

FEED ME

Add a high-potash fertilizer to my water two or three times in the growing period (spring and summer).

HELP ME FLOWER

Keep me healthy to encourage my clusters of pinkish-red flowers. These grow from the ends of my hanging stems in early summer.

SHARE ME

Share me in spring or summer by cutting off one of my stems. Trim it into pieces about 7cm (2¾in) long, and lay them on dry compost with a thin layer of sand. Water once roots start to appear.

REPOT ME

Repot me very carefully into a slightly larger hanging pot in early spring. Use dry compost, and don't water me for a week or two afterwards.

I come from Mexico and Honduras.

POSITION ME

Give me a place to grow in partial shade so that full sun does not damage my leaves.

TOP FIVE...
EASY-SHARERS

Many cacti and succulents can be easily propagated (see pp.26–27) from offsets or cuttings. These new plants can make great gifts or additions to your collection.

1 **BLACK ROSE**
Aeonium arboreum
atropurpureum 'Zwartkop'
You can propagate this popular succulent from stem cuttings, taken in spring and summer.
See Black rose, pp.34–35.

2 **TIGER ALOE**
Aloe variegata
This little succulent produces offset rosettes. These can be gently removed when repotting to create new plants.
See Tiger aloe, pp.38–39.

3 CHRISTMAS CACTUS
Schlumbergera truncata

This winter-flowering cactus can be propagated from cuttings taken at the stem joints. These should then be placed in compost to encourage root growth.

See Christmas cactus, pp.128–29.

4 SILVER CROWN
Cotyledon undulata

Silver crown succulent can be propagated from cuttings taken just below the bottom leaves. Take care when handling, as the white, dusty leaves are easily marked.

See Silver crown, pp.48–49.

5 CROWN CACTUS
Rebutia krainziana

Offsets can be removed from this plant when they are at least 2cm (¾in) tall. These should be left to dry for a week before potting.

See Crown cactus, pp.124–25.

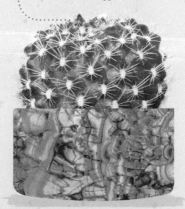

STRING OF BEADS

Senecio rowleyanus

This trailing succulent makes a fascinating, low-maintenance houseplant for a hanging basket, with its pea-sized leaves on long, trailing stems.

|||||||||||||||||||||||||||||||||||||||||||||||||||||||||||||||||||||||||||||||||||||

VITAL STATISTICS

- **HOW IT GROWS** String of beads has stems that multiply and lengthen to cascade over the sides of its pot.

SHADIER SPOT

Don't expose string of beads to too much direct sunlight as it may scorch. Just move it to a shadier spot if this occurs.

- **ANATOMY** The stems of this trailing plant are covered with round, green leaves that resemble peas or beads. These have a smaller surface area than a flat leaf, which helps the plant store water and not lose moisture to dry air.

- **SIZE** The stems can grow to about 1m (3ft) in length. In bright, but not too sunny conditions, they may grow 20–25cm (8–10in) per year. They can be trimmed back as necessary (and the ends used for cuttings).

Indoors: 1m (3ft)

WATER ME

Water me every couple of weeks in spring and summer. Don't water me at all from mid-autumn to spring.

POSITION ME

Pot me in a hanging basket near a moderately sunny window, with not too much direct sun.

SHARE ME

In early summer, cut off a length of my stem with a sharp knife or scissors and cut it into pieces about 5cm (2in) long. Lay these on fresh soil with a thin layer of sand. Water them only when roots appear.

HELP ME FLOWER

With the right amount of light, water, and food, in summer I produce white tubular flowers from my thin stems. My flowers have a pleasant, slightly spicy scent.

FEED ME

Add a high-potash fertilizer to my water two or three times in spring and summer.

I come from South Africa.

REPOT ME

Move me to a slightly larger pot in early spring. Gather my stems lightly together when repotting me. Use dry compost and only water me after about two weeks.

BRAIN CACTUS

Stenocactus crispatus

From a genus formerly known as Echinofossulocactus, the brain cactus combines wavy ribs with bold spines and intricate flowers.

VITAL STATISTICS

- **HOW IT GROWS** The brain cactus forms a solitary stem that is rounded in shape or that forms a short column.

SORE POINT

This cactus has strong spines that will penetrate the thickest gloves, so handle it with extra care when repotting.

- **ANATOMY** The narrow, wavy ribs, which give the brain cactus its name, can make it hard to remove mealybugs (see pp.28–29). The pale, flat spines can be up to 1cm (½in) long. The flowers appear on top of the stem in spring and summer.

- **SIZE** *Stenocactus* are slow growing, even in the wild. They grow into a short column about 12cm (5in) tall and 10cm (4in) wide after ten or more years. They may eventually produce offsets if repotted regularly.

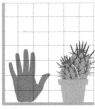

Indoors: 12cm (5in)

WATER ME

Water me every two weeks or so in spring and summer, but only when my compost is nearly dry. Don't water me at all from mid-autumn to early spring.

POSITION ME

Ensure that I have a sunny spot on a windowsill or in a greenhouse kept above 5°C (41°F).

FEED ME
Give me a high-potash fertilizer two or three times during the growing period.

SHARE ME
I am slow to make clusters, so you may have to wait until I produce offsets (young plants) that can be removed. I can also be grown from seed (see p.27).

HELP ME FLOWER
If I have plenty of sun, my white and purple flowers appear in the centre of my new growth when I am a few years old.

REPOT ME
Find me a new pot before watering starts in early spring. Put me into dry compost in a slightly larger pot and water only after two weeks.

I come from Mexico.

SULCOREBUTIA
Sulcorebutia rauschii

Although recently combined with Rebutia, another genus known for producing beautiful flowers, many experts still consider Sulcorebutia a separate genus.

VITAL STATISTICS

● **HOW IT GROWS** *Sulcorebutia rauschii* is globular, growing slowly to make a cluster of purple and green stems.

WHAT'S IN A NAME?
Sulcorebutia rauschii is named after its first collector – Walter Rausch – who discovered it on a mountain in Bolivia.

● **ANATOMY** Individual stems vary from 2–4cm (¾–1½in) in height and slightly wider in diameter. They cluster tightly together to form a clump. The groups of spines are short, black, and look like a fishbone. Deep pink flowers emerge from the base.

WATER ME
Water me every two weeks or so in spring and summer when the compost is nearly dry. Don't water me at all in late autumn and winter.

● **SIZE** This species can spread with offsets (young plants) to make a clump about 15–20cm (6–8in) across after eight or ten years if repotted regularly and cared for well. The spread is indefinite.

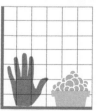

Indoors: 20cm (8in) across

POSITION ME
Place me in a sunny spot on a windowsill or in a greenhouse with a minimum temperature of 4° C (39° F).

SHARE ME

Remove my offsets in early summer when they are at least 2cm (¾in) tall. Cut them at the junction with the main stem, dry them for a week, then place them on fresh, dry compost with a layer of sand. Water them once new roots appear.

HELP ME FLOWER

I need good exposure to sunlight to keep me healthy and encourage my pink flowers. My stems produce these flowers around the base in late spring.

MEET THE RELATIVES

SULCOREBUTIA ARENACEA
This globular cactus is yellow-green and has about 30 ribs in a spiral arrangement. It has large, yellow flowers.

REPOT ME

Move me during spring into a slightly larger pot of dry, fresh compost. Don't water me for two weeks.

I come from Bolivia.

FEED ME

Add a high-potash fertilizer to my water two or three times in the growing period (spring and summer).

SULCOREBUTIA HERTUSII
Like its relative, this cactus produces pink flowers. It is slow-growing, clustering, and has distinctive hair-like spines covering its body.

GLORY OF TEXAS
Thelocactus bicolor

This is the best-known member of a genus comprising only about a dozen plants. It has striking funnel-shaped flowers.

VITAL STATISTICS

- **HOW IT GROWS** Glory of Texas grows slowly to form a cluster of either globular or short, columnar stems.

GET GLOVED UP!
Wear thick gloves when repotting this plant as it has particularly long, sharp spines.

- **ANATOMY** The spines, which vary from dark brown to whitish yellow, grow along the spirally arranged ribs. The real "glories" of this species, however, are the large pink flowers that appear from the growing point at the top of the stem.

- **SIZE** Glory of Texas – along with most other plants in the *Thelocactus* genus – grows to a maximum height of about 12–15cm (5–6in).

Indoors: 12–15cm (5–6in)

WATER ME
Give me a drink every two weeks or so, when my soil is nearly dry – but only during the spring and summer growing season.

POSITION ME
I will thrive in a sunny spot, such as on a south-facing windowsill or in a greenhouse with a sunny aspect.

HELP ME FLOWER

I should flower without any special help when I'm a few years old – provided I'm exposed to enough direct sunlight.

SHARE ME

It might be best to keep me to yourself or grow another plant from seed (see p.27), as taking cuttings from this and other plants in the genus can easily cause damage.

REPOT ME

This is best done in early spring, before watering starts again. Use dry compost and a slightly bigger pot.

FEED ME

Add a high-potash fertilizer to my water two or three times in spring and summer.

I come from Mexico and Texas, USA.

(see p.27)

MEET THE RELATIVES

THELOCACTUS BUEKII

This species has similar care needs to the glory of Texas. It has large, purplish pink flowers and comes from Nuevo León, Mexico.

THELOCACTUS HEXAEDROPHORUS

Native to Mexico, this is a widespread member of the Thelocactus genus. It typically produces white, funnel-shaped flowers and requires the same care as glory of Texas.

INDEX

|||||||||||||||||||||||||||||||||||||||||||||||||||||||||||||||||||||||||||||||||||||||||||

ABOUT THE CONSULTANT

John Pilbeam has been growing, studying, visiting in the wild, and writing about cacti and succulents for over half a century. John has published more than 20 books – and numerous articles for specialist journals – on many different genera, as well as giving talks to enthusiasts in the UK, Ireland, USA, Canada, Mexico, Australia, France, Germany, Belgium, Netherlands, and Italy.

ACKNOWLEDGMENTS

Consultant: For their help and encouragement in various ways during the gestation of this book, I would like to thank fellow members of the *British Cactus & Succulent Society*: Ralph Northcott, Derek Bowdery, David Neville, Mike Partridge, Tony Roberts, Graham Charles, Jean Forward, Diane Walpole, Sylvia Porter, Elizabeth Maddock, Hazel Taylor, Alain Sutton; and to John Trager of *The Cactus & Succulent Society of America*, as well as to the authors and compilers of *The New Cactus Lexicon* (David Hunt) and the six volumes of *The Illustrated Handbook of Succulent Plants* (Urs Eggli).

Publisher: DK would like to thank US consultant Jeff Moore at Solana Succulents; Jane Simmonds for proofreading; Vanessa Bird for creating the index; and Sunil Sharma, Rajdeep Singh, Satish Gaur, and Manish Upreti at DK Delhi for DTP work. We would also like to thank Ralph Northcott at cactusshop.co.uk for allowing us to take photos of the plants at his nursery, and for his help and expertise during photography.

Picture credits: The publisher would like to thank the following for their kind permission to reproduce their photographs:

(Key: a-above; b-below/bottom; c-centre; f-far; l-left; r-right; t-top)

Depositphotos Inc: Tamara_k 4cr, 5cr, 6clb, 7cr, 8cra, 9cb, 10cra, 11crb, 19clb, 76-77bc, 80bl, 90-91bc, 101clb, 126br; Dreamstime.com: Designprintck 10bc, 122-123bc, Fotoeye75 6ca, 6c (Dirt), 6cr, 6bc, 8crb, 9cla, 10crb, 20crb, 58-59c, 59cra, 59crb, 81crb, 86-87c, Halyna Kavun / Kavunchik 5cra, 5clb, 7c, 10cb, 11bl, 14bc, 16bl, 29br, 34-35bc, 35cra, 35crb, 38-39bc, 39cra, 39crb, 53c, 67clb, 80cr, 82-83bc, 83cra, 83crb, 101cra, 102-103bc, 103cra, 103crb, 127clb, 128-129bc, 129cra, 132crb, Katyshka 6crb, 8bc (terracotta), 9ca, 11ca, 15br, 18crb, 25cra, 25crb, 36-37bc, 37cra, 37crb, 52bl, 64-65bc, 66br, 101cla, 109bl, 127crb, 140-141bc, 141cra, 141crb,

Liligraphie 5br, 9bl, 10tr, 42-43bc, 43cra, 43crb, Sailorman 6cla, 17crb, 26c, 48-49bc, 49cra, 49crb, 81cla, 96-97bc, 133bl, Surachet Khamsuk / Surachetkhamsuk 8cla, 9cb (Silver), 40-41bc, 41cra, 41crb, Veronika Surovtseva / surovtseva 9cl, 10br, 11tc, 11ca (concrete), 98-99bc, 108cr, 127cra, 135cl, Thanarit Manyamin / Thanarit 4c, 6c, 7cla, 7br, 14cr, 19cla, 26br, 32-33bc, 33cra, 52crb, 67cla, 84-85bc, 85cra, 85crb, 106-107bc, 107cra, 107crb, Ukrphoto 6bc (Malachite), 7cb, 9crb, 10clb, 11cra, 11bc, 133br, 138-139bc, 139crb, Victor Torres / Somatuscani 1, 3, 7ca, 10cb (Orange Stucco), 11cra (Orange Stucco), Wangyun 8cb, 10cla, 14bl, 21bc, 62-63bc, 63cra, 63crb, 92-93bc, 93cra, 93crb, Willds 21c, 53br, 118-119bc, 119cra, 119crb, Natalia Zakharova 5bc, 7ca (striped), 8bc, 9clb, 9br, 11cla, 15bl, 16cr, 50-51bc, 51cra, 51crb, 70-71bc, 100br, 110-111bc, 124-125bc; Elizabeth Maddock 130-131c

Cover images: Front: Dreamstime.com: Victor Torres / Somatuscani cr; Back: Dreamstime.com: Fotoeye75 ca, Halyna Kavun / Kavunchik cra, Sailorman cla, Victor Torres / Somatuscani ca/ (Orange Stucco); Spine: Dreamstime.com: Fotoeye75 cb, Sailorman bc, Victor Torres / Somatuscani

Endpaper images: Front: Dreamstime.com: Halyna Kavun / Kavunchik tc (Gold metallic), fcr, bc, Jolin fcla, cra, c (pink granite), clb, Ovydyborets tc, ca (paper), cl, cb (paper), bc (paper), fbr, Sailorman tr, c, bl, bc (Layered sandstone), Veronika Surovtseva / surovtseva ftr, cla, ca (grunge concrete), fclb, cb (grunge concrete), Ukrphoto tc (Malachite), cb (Malachite), fbl, Victor Torres / Somatuscani tc (Orange Stucco), fcra, fcl, c (Orange Stucco), cb, fcrb, Willds tc (Steel Metal), ca, cr, br;

All images © Dorling Kindersley

For further information see: www.dkimages.com

WARNING

Euphorbia sap, which may ooze from a plant if accidentally knocked or damaged, is harmful if it comes into contact with tender parts of the body – particularly the eyes, nose, and mouth. If this occurs, immediately wash the affected areas with copious amounts of water. Always take care when handling cacti and succulents – especially *Opuntias* – and wear gloves if necessary.